Lectionary Worship Aids

For use with the Common Lectionary

Series A

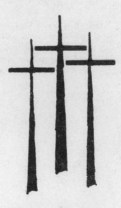

Heth H. Corl

C.S.S. Worship Resources Library

Copyright © 1986 by
The C.S.S. Publishing Company, Inc.
Lima, Ohio

6843 / ISBN 0-89536-814-5

To Beki

TABLE OF CONTENTS

Easter Season

Season of Pentecost

PUBLISHER'S PREFACE

The worship elements provided in **Lectionary Worship Aids — Series A** are offered by the C.S.S. Publishing Company as resources to enrich the worship experience for those who utilize them.

Although this volume is copyrighted, the publishers will permit the printing or mimeographing of any elements contained herein, when the printing or mimeographing is for use during a worship service. All other reproduction is, of course, protected by the copyright.

We hope that your use of these materials will prove beneficial in your worship.

The C.S.S Publishing Company

Foreword

The increasing use during the past fifteen years of the various denominational versions of the three-year ecumenical lectionary has now resulted in a second generation ecumenical lectionary. The Common Lectionary, as it is called, reduces to a minimum the denominational variations in the lectionary and responds to criticisms of the lectionary that have been received, especially its use of the Old Testament.

One of the advantages of the three-year lectionary has been the wealth of worship and preaching resources which it has stimulated. Creative ministers have not only been helped to plan their own congregation's worship, they have also been able to publish what they have done, so that other ministers might benefit from their creativity.

Heth Corl is a fine example of such a creative minister. His LECTIONARY WORSHIP AIDS has been a useful resource ever since it was first published, and now in revised form it will be more helpful than ever. The three sets of resources for every Sunday not only give the minister a wide range of choice for Sunday morning, they also provide resources for the church that has additional services Sunday evening or midweek.

It is my hope that ministers using these resources will be free and creative enough to choose what best fits the realities of their local situations, to make adaptations, adn to be prompted by these examples to develop their own ideas and acts of worship. Perhaps out of this collection will come resources written by others that can be, in turn, published and shared. Through this process of sharing, ministers and congregations who wish vital and creative worship stand greatly to benefit.

Hoyt L. Hickman
Section on Worship
Board of Discipleship
The United Methodist Church

INTRODUCTION

This new set of LECTIONARY WORSHIP AIDS has been revised to correspond with Common Lectionary. The three-year lectionary prepared by the Consultation on Church Union in 1974 became widely used throughout many denominations. However, there were some problems inherent, so that to make the lectionary as ecumenical as the denominations using it, a revision was necessary. Variations in the dating system for the Sundays after Pentecost had not been dealt with in the lectionary. The Old Testament lessons had been chosen primarily to correspond with the Gospel, limiting the message of the Old Testament. Verses within the lections varied from t a few to many.

Consequently, teh Consultation on Common Texts created the North American Committee on Calendar and Lectionary in 1978, to develop a consensus lectionary. It is this lectionary for which Lectionary Worship Aids has been revised.

The Gospel lessons have remained basically unchanged. The greatest changes have been made in the Old Testament lessons. Many of the lections have been changed only by the specific verses selected. New Year's Day and Thanksgiving have been added to the lectionary, as have additional readings for Christmas Eve/Day. there is now agreement on dating the Sundays after Pentecost.

Whether or not your congregation follows the lectionary, these worship resources can be helpful in preparing a worship service. All Scriptures used in these resources have been indexed. Begin with the Scriptures you have selected for a particular service. If that Scripture is listed in the index of Scriptures, it will refer to resources based on that text which may be appropriate, even though that text has been selected for a different Sunday of the Christian Year. The same thing can be done with the Topical Index.

These resources provide continuity in the service of worship by following the theme derived from the lesson selected for the day. Each lection has three lessons: The First Lesson, an Old Testament reading except when Acts is read during the Easter Season; the Second Lesson, one of the New Testament books other than the Gospels; and the Gospel. A set of resources is provided for each of the three lessons, even though only one will be used for a given service. Thus for each service, a pastor may choose to read all three lessons from the lection, but use only the resources for the lesson from which he or she chooses a text for the sermon.

The resources are also biblical. They are based on Scripture, but are not quotations of Scripture. A variety of translations and commentaries was used in an exegetical study to develop resources that would be true to the Scripture being read and interpreted in the act of worship.

The resources are of a length which permits them to be mimeographed in a regular size bulletin using elite type. A worship service using the Call to Worship, Collect, and Prayer of Confession can be typed on the inside pages in the order of service, allowing the back page to be used for concerns of the congregation.

Each church is accustomed to its own order of service. The use of these resources does not need to change that order. However, they have been written from a point of view which interprets the act of worship through this general outline:

- God calls us to worship him.
- We respond with praise and thanksgiving.
- God speaks to us through his Word.
- Hearing that Word, we confess our sins.
- Assured of our forgiveness, we give ourselves in dedication.
- We then intercede on behalf of others.
- The order concludes with God's departing blessing.

This order places the Prayer of Confession after the sermon which lifts up a particular area in which we need to examine ourselves. We then confess our failure in that area, followed by a dedication of ourselves in discipleship in that particular area. An order which places the Prayer of Confession earlier in the service would not limit the use of these resources.

I am grateful to Hoyt L. Hickman, Edwin E. Burtner, and James F. White, all of whom gave valuable advice int he development and writing of these worship aids. I am also indebted to my wife, Karen, for typing the manuscript.

It is my hope that these aids to worship will assist congregations in expressing their worship of God with words which speak on their behalf in ways that are true to their faith.

— Heth H. Corl

FIRST SUNDAY IN ADVENT

First Lesson: Isaiah 2:1-5
Theme: Peace in God's Kingdom

Call to Worship
Pastor: Peace is the gift God offers to our world. But only those who walk in his paths shall find it.
People: We have come to the Lord's house; that he may teach us his ways, and that we may walk in his paths.
Pastor: If we will walk in his paths, he will teach us to turn our acts of violence into expressions of peace.
People: We do not want to learn the way of war. May the peace of God be our way of life.

Collect
O gracious Father, who knows our warring nature, and comes to teach us the way of peace: Come to us anew in the Spirit of Christ; that his advent in our hearts will bring peace on earth and goodwill among men. In our Savior's name we pray. Amen.

Prayer of Confession
We have the mental capacity to want peace, Father; but in our hearts are the battlefields where we destroy the desire of our minds. By nature we become living amunition, the visible expression of what we think in our hearts. Forgive us for our self-centeredness that has made us skilled warriors doomed to be defeated by that very skill. Draw us into your presence; that we may learn your ways, walk in your paths, and live in your peace; through Christ our Lord. Amen.

Hymns
"Come Down, O Love Divine"
"Lead Us, O Father"
"O For a Closer Walk with God"
"Walk in the Light"

FIRST SUNDAY IN ADVENT

Second Lesson: Romans 13:11-14
Theme: Living in the Light of Christ

Call to Worship

Pastor: As winter sets in, the days are shorter and we live in more darkness.

People: Sometimes we feel that life has its wintertime, too, in which darkness steals the light by which we live.

Pastor: Then you can rejoice! For darkness turns to light as we make ready for the advent of Christ, the Light of the world!

People: We want to cast off the works of darkness in our lives, and put on the armor of Christ our light!

Collect

Eternal Father, whose advent is like the beginning of a new day: Give us the desire to turn from the darkness of sin: that we may see the glory of a new day with Christ, the Light of our lives, through whom we pray. Amen.

Prayer of Confession

O God our Father, we look at ourselves at the beginning of this Advent season, only to admit we have enjoyed the darkness too long. We shy away from the brilliance of Christ, because we are ashamed of what it reveals in us. Forgive us for our sinful ways. As we prepare for Christ's coming, help us to begin a new day with you; all darkness dispelled, Christ being the joy of our lives. In his name we pray. Amen.

Hymns

"Break Forth, O Living Light"
"I Heard the Voice of Jesus Say"
"Lead Kindly Light"
"O Son of God Incarnate"

FIRST SUNDAY IN ADVENT

Gospel: Matthew 24:36-44
Theme: Watch in readiness for Christ

Call to Worship

Pastor: God's future plans for us are unknown: but we do know the future is in his hands.

People: We know the future is in God's hands; and that is where we want to be also.

Pastor: We do not need to fear. If we are alert to God's will for us; and commit our lives to him, our future will have his blessing.

People: We face the future with faith, not with fear; because we trust God to fulfill history in his own way and time.

Collect

Eternal God, whose mercy has allowed us to hear your good news of salvation before our Lord's final advent: Give us sensitive hearts and minds to live a new life; that we may not be found unprepared when you call us into eternity. We pray through Christ our Lord. Amen.

Prayer of Confession

If we knew when Christ would return, Father; we would feel more comfortable. But we do not know; and we become careless in living responsible lives. Forgive us for weak commitment based on our manipulation of faith and hope. Give us the desire to surrender our total being without the necessity of knowing when the day of our Lord will come; but only that each day requires us to live our best. In our Savior's name we pray. Amen.

Hymns

"Come, Thou Long Expected Jesus"
"God of Our Life"
"I Know Not What the Future Hath"
"Lord, It Belongs Not to My Care"

SECOND SUNDAY IN ADVENT

First Lesson: Isaiah 11:1-10
Theme: The Messiah is endowed with God's Spirit

Call to Worship

Pastor: Of all the descendants of King David, only Jesus fulfills Israel's messianic hope.

People: Jesus is God's Son, endowed with God's Spirit to be our Savior.

Pastor: Our Lord judges with righteousness; that we may acknowledge God's sovereignty in our lives.

People: We accept with gladness the righteous judgment of Christ our Lord, and the sovereign rule of God our Father.

Collect

Almighty God, whose Son, Jesus, fulfills the ancient hope of a Messiah empowered by your Spirit: Make us responsive to his advent in our lives; that we may learn to acknowledge you as our God and Father, and enjoy the blessedness of your kingdom. In our Savior's name we pray. Amen.

Prayer of Confession

Heavenly Father, our hope is in your only Son, Jesus our Savior, who was born to bring peace and justice to our world. We want the kingdom which he announced; but we confess we have not fulfilled our responsibilities as citizens of that kingdom. Forgive us for our resistance to acknowledge your sovereignty in our lives. May our Advent celebrations bring us into a closer relationship with you, that we may be filled with your knowledge. We pray in Jesus' name. Amen.

Hymns

"All Hail the Power of Jesus' Name"
"Hail to the Lord's Anointed"
"O Morning Star, How Fair and Bright"
"O Spirit of the Living God"

SECOND SUNDAY IN ADVENT

Second Lesson: Romans 15:4-13
Theme: Scripture was written that we might have hope

Call to Worship

Pastor: God inspired men of old to record his Word, that we might have hope.
People: Our hope is in Christ, who came in fulfillment of God's promises in his Word.
Pastor: Our hope continues to grow because Christ has assured us that our future is also in God's hands.
People: We commit ourselves to study God's Word, that hope may continue to grow in us.

Collect

Eternal God, you who are true to your promises recorded in the Scriptures: Instill in our hearts a greater desire to read and study your Word; that by the power of the Holy Spirit, hope may strengthen our faith. We pray through Christ, the hope of the world. Amen.

Prayer of Confession

Your Word is precious to us, Father. But we confess we are not as familiar with your promises as we ought to be. Forgive us for limiting our hope by not being better students of Scripture. May our study of your Word lead us to a knowledge and acceptance of your Son as Lord and Savior. In his name we pray. Amen.

Hymns

"Book of Books, Our People's Strength"
"Hope of the World"
"My Hope Is Built"
"O Word of God Incarnate"

SECOND SUNDAY IN ADVENT

Gospel: Matthew 3:1-12
Theme: The call to repentance

Call to Worship

Pastor: Advent is a call to repentance in preparation for Jesus' ministry of salvation.

People: Many of us are baptized Christians. But there is still a need for change in our lives.

Pastor: Jesus comes to baptize us with the Holy Spirit; and that calls for a life style which gives evidence of repentance.

People: We commit ourselves to new life in Christ, assured that he will enable us with the Holy Spirit to live that life.

Collect

Merciful Father, who calls us into repentance not only with our lips, but with our lives: Direct us into a new life of righteousness through sincere repentance; that we may accept our Lord's ministry as our source of strength and salvation. In our Savior's name we pray. Amen.

Prayer of Confession

Our Father, we preserve our certificates of baptism as proof of our allegiance to Christ; but our lives do not show that we have turned from our sins. Forgive us for our superficial loyalty which prevents you from inspiring us with the Holy Spirit. Come to our aid; that we may feel your Spirit strengthening us in the life revealed through Christ our Savior; in whose name we pray. Amen.

Hymns

"Come, Every Soul by Sin Oppressed"
"Come, Thou Long-Expected Jesus"
"I Know Not How That Bethlehem's Babe"
"There's a Voice in the Wilderness Crying"

THIRD SUNDAY IN ADVENT

First Lesson: Isaiah 35:1-10
Theme: Rejoice, God is coming to save us!

Call to Worship

Pastor: The advent of Christ brings the joy of God's presence in our midst!

People: We sing praises to God for the salvation Christ brings to us!

Pastor: Because of Christ, the weak are strengthened; the fearful are encouraged; and the unrighteous are redeemed!

People: Joy and gladness are ours, because God has come to us in Christ to walk with us in the paths of righteousness!

Collect

Gracious Father, who is ever in the process of coming to your children to make straight their paths, to heal their infirmities, and to forgive their sins: Give us the joyful assurance of your continuing advent in our lives; that we may live the life in which we can sing the glad songs of salvation. We pray through Christ our Redeemer. Amen.

Prayer of Confession

We wander so easily, Father, from the paths of righteousness. We long for your intervention which will create a new road for us to find our way into your gracious love and redemption. Forgive us for our fears, insecurities, and sins which have kept us from having a closer walk with you. Come to us in the advent of your Son; that we may be reborn to joy and gladness. In his name we pray. Amen.

Hymns

"Lead Us, O Father"
"O For a Closer Walk with God"
"Rejoice, Ye Pure in Heart"
"When We Walk with the Lord"

THIRD SUNDAY IN ADVENT

Second Lesson: James 5:7-10
Theme: Be patient until the Lord comes

Call to Worship

Pastor: Christ was born in humility and served in meekness but he promised to return in glorious majesty.

People: We rejoice in the birth of our Savior, and await the day when he will return.

Pastor: We do not know when that day will be; but we are told to be patient until he comes, and keep our hope high.

People: We celebrate the birth of our Lord who has promised to return to rule the world in justice and righteousness.

Collect

Almighty God, whose Son was born of lowly birth, and who gave his life in humble service to die upon a cross for our redemption: Keep hope alive in us as we wait patiently for him; that our lives may not deny the salvation he brought with his birth. In his name we pray. Amen.

Prayer of Confession

Dear Father, we are enthused about the birth of Jesus, our Lord. But we tend to see his lordship only within the limits of his birth and resurrection. We are not as excited about his promise to return in judgment. Forgive us for building our faith more on the glory of the past than on the hope of the future. Help us to live expectantly in the assurance that he who came to earth in fulfillment of your promise, shall also fulfill your promise with his return. In our Savior's name we pray. Amen.

Hymns

"Lord Christ, When First Thou Cam'st"
"O Day of God, Draw Nigh"
"The King Shall Come"

THIRD SUNDAY IN ADVENT

Gospel: Matthew 11:2-11
Theme: Jesus is the Messiah

Call to Worship

Pastor: We have twenty centuries of church history giving evidence that Jesus is the Christ, the promised Messiah.

People: We have heard from others, and we have seen for ourselves, what wonderful things God does through his Son Jesus, our Savior.

Pastor: Truly, God is present in his Son to heal the brokenness of his world!

People: Jesus is our Lord, the Messiah who brings God's salvation to us!

Collect

Eternal God, who reveals to each generation your saving grace in Jesus Christ your Son: Prevent our hearts and minds from any doubts about this babe of Bethlehem; that we may rejoice in the good news of salvation which he brings. In our Savior's name we pray. Amen.

Prayer of Confession

We believe Jesus is the Christ, the promised Messiah, Father. But that confession is more a memorized creed than an experience of faith. Forgive us when we confuse the fallacy of childhood fantasies with the beautiful story of redemption. Open our eyes to the wonderful signs of your glorious presence in the ministry of our Savior; that our faith may not falter by any doubts. We pray in his name. Amen.

Hymns

"Hail to the Lord's Anointed"
"Let All Mortal Flesh Keep Silence"
"Love Divine, All Loves Excelling"
"O Son of God Incarnate"

FOURTH SUNDAY IN ADVENT

First Lesson: Isaiah 7:10-16
Theme: God is with his people.

Call to Worship

Pastor: God intervenes in history to prove he is with his people, acting on their behalf.

People: God has done that quite often; but the greatest sign of his presence is the birth of Christ.

Pastor: Jesus was called Emmanuel, because he was living evidence that God had come to save his people.

People: He is our Emmanuel, too! For God is with us in his Son who came to be our Savior!

Collect

O loving God, who makes your presence felt in each generation, blessing your people with grace and guidance: May the gift of your Son, acknowledged through our celebration of his birth, be the sign of your presence in our generation; that we may know you are in our midst to save us. In his name we pray. Amen.

Prayer of Confession

The songs of Christmas are so familiar to us, Father; but in the rush of busy schedules, we become numb to their message that you have come to live in our midst. Forgive us when we are insensitive to your presence, and unresponsive to your life. Awaken us to your presence in the birth of your Son; that we may live our lives in the assurance that you are always with us. We pray through Christ our Savior. Amen.

Hymns

"Angels, from the Realms of Glory"
"Let All Together Praise Our God"
"Love Came Down at Christmas"
"O Little Town of Bethlehem"

FOURTH SUNDAY IN ADVENT

Second Lesson: Romans 1:1-7
Theme: Jesus: Son of God, son of man

Call to Worship

Pastor: What a wonderful Savior is Jesus our Lord!
People: He is Son of God, and son of man.
Pastor: In the flesh he suffered all the trials of man; yet as Son of God, he brought salvation for all mankind.
People: Jesus is Lord! We give him our lives in thanksgiving for his gift of new life.

Collect

Almighty God, whose good news is the gift of your Son who was born of woman: Convict us of our need to accept him as our Savior, that we may share in the blessings of the life you give through him. In his name we pray. Amen.

Prayer of Confession

We are very conscious of the gift of your Son, Father. We rejoice with others in the celebration of his birth. But our celebration is more a party, than putting into practice the new way of life which he taught. Forgive us for hearing the good news, but not living the good life that is proclaimed in the news. Help us to see in your Son, one who lived in the flesh, that we may follow his example of living the righteous life. We pray in the name of Christ, our Lord. Amen.

Hymns

"Hail to the Lord's Anointed"
"Hark! the Herald Angels Sing"
"Let All Together Praise Our God"
"Love Came Down at Christmas"

FOURTH SUNDAY IN ADVENT

Gospel: Matthew 1:18-25
Theme: Jesus' divine origin

Call to Worship

Pastor: Long ago God promised a Messiah whose mission would be to make God's presence a reality.

People: God revealed to Joseph in a dream that Mary's son was to be that Messiah.

Pastor: Jesus' birth is divine, because God intervened in history to send his Son.

People: God continues to give himself through his Son; that all who recognize his divine origin may find him to be their Emmanuel.

Collect

Almighty God, whose order in creation makes every birth a miracle; but who ordered Jesus' birth to be uniquely divine: Become real in our lives as we put our faith in Jesus your Son; that we may know you have come to be with us in everyday life. We pray in Jesus' name. Amen.

Prayer of Confession

We come with joy in our hearts, Father, because we know Jesus came to save us from our sins. We invite you to be our Emmanuel, and ask that you forgive us our sins through Jesus, your Son. May the joy we feel at his birth increase as we grow in our commitment to him who has brought your love to us. We pray through Christ our Lord. Amen.

Hymns

"O Little Town of Bethlehem"
"Silent Night, Holy Night"
"There's a Song in the Air"
"What Child Is This"

CHRISTMAS EVE/DAY
(First Option)

First Lesson: Isaiah 9:2-7
Theme: Unto us a child is born

Call to Worship

Pastor: Rejoice! For God's light has come to dispel our darkness!

People: We rejoice as those who reap a great harvest. For God has sent his Son to be our Savior!

Pastor: There is no end to the justice and righteousness of his kingdom which is for every one who will let him rule in their hearts.

People: We bow before Christ our Lord, born to deliver us from the oppression of sin!

Collect

O God of love and peace, whose Son transforms our darkness into light, and our sadness into joy: Cleanse our hearts of all sin and unrighteousness; that Christ may be born in us, and rule in our hearts. We pray in our Savior's name. Amen.

Prayer of Confession

We praise you, O God, for the Prince of Peace, your only Son, Jesus our Savior, whose birth gives reason for our joyful adoration on this holy day. Forgive us for our sins which have defeated us in life, taking control of our thoughts, our words, and our actions. Grant us deliverance as the Christ child is enthroned in our hearts to be our ruler and Savior. In his name we pray. Amen.

Hymns

"All My Heart This Night Rejoices"
"Angels, from the Realms of Glory"
"Joy to the World"
"The People That in Darkness Sat"

CHRISTMAS EVE/DAY
(First Option)

Second Lesson: Titus 2:11-14
Theme: Live godly lives in preparation for Christ's return

Call to Worship

Pastor: God's grace has become known through the gift of his Son, Jesus our Savior.

People: We celebrate our Savior's birth, and rejoice in the hope he has brought us.

Pastor: Jesus came in the flesh to help us live godly lives, that our hope may be fulfilled when he returns in glory.

People: Our hope is not only in his birth, but in his glory as Son of God, Savior of the world.

Collect

O God our Father, who by your grace has brought us deliverance from sin through your only Son, Jesus our Lord: Inspire us by your saving grace to live godly lives, that we may share in the glory of your Son when he returns. In his name we pray. Amen.

Prayer of Confession

Father, we celebrate our Savior's birth; but we do it by looking back in history. We have difficulty looking to the future, knowing this same Jesus will return in glory. Forgive us for our sins which threaten us, filling us with fear when we think of our Lord's return. Fill us with joy that causes us to celebrate not only the babe of Bethlehem, but also the Christ who is to come. We pray in his name. Amen.

Hymns

"Lo, He Comes with Clouds Descending"
"Lord Christ, When First Thou Cam'st"
"O Day of God, Draw Nigh"
"The King Shall Come"

CHRISTMAS EVE/DAY
(First Option)

Gospel: Gospel Luke 2 1-20
Theme: Good news! Salvation is here!

Call to Worship

Pastor: God in his great love has given his Son to be our Savior!

People: The good news of God's love fills our hearts with joy!

Pastor: Salvation has come, and is available to all who will receive Jesus as Lord and Savior.

People: We worship our Savior, and commit ourselves to the way of peace proclaimed at his birth.

Collect

Father in heaven, who gave your only Son to be our Savior, that we might learn the way of peace: Let the joy with which we celebrate his birth stir us into a deeper commitment of Christian living; that peace may come, not only to our hearts, but to our world. In our Savior's name we pray. Amen.

Prayer of Confession

With great joy we lift our hearts in praise, O God, for the gift of your Son! We join the throngs who hail your Son as Savior of the world. But our praise is too shallow, and too brief. Soon we will be weary; and our joy will fall like the needles of a pine tree, cut from its roots. Forgive us for whatever is superficial in our celebration of your Son's birth. Remove the disguises we wear this time of year; and let your good news of salvation get through to our hearts. We pray in Jesus' name. Amen.

Hymns

"Infant Holy, Infant Lowly"
"It Came Upon the Midnight Clear"
"Joy to the World"
"While Shepherds Watched Their Flocks"

CHRISTMAS EVE/DAY
(Second Option)

First Lesson: Isaiah 62:6-7, 10-12
Theme: The joy of salvation

Call to Worship

Pastor: Open your hearts, my friends. Let salvation enter.

People: God has sent his Son to save us! We are God's people because he has redeemed us.

Pastor: The Savior is born. Let the whole world know that God loves his people, and rejoice.

People: Joy is bursting our hearts! May all who hear of our Savior's birth prepare for his redeeming love.

Collect

Gracious God, who fills our hearts with the joy of salvation through the birth of your Son: Let the glad songs we sing fill the air; that our world may hear, and receive the salvation your Son has brought to all who will receive him. In his name we pray. Amen.

Prayer of Confession

It is easy, Lord, to sing from memory, and rejoice from habit when we celebrate Christmas. Often our hearts are crowded with concerns contrary to our Savior's birth. Forgive us when our praises become impersonal replays of prepared rituals. Let the songs we sing and the joy we share come from our hearts in response to the salvation you have given to us through your Son, Jesus Christ, in whose name we pray. Amen.

Hymns

"All My Heart This Night Rejoices"
"Good Christian Men, Rejoice"
"Joy To The World"
"Let All Together Praise Our God"

CHRISTMAS EVE/DAY
(Second Option)

Second Lesson: Titus 3:4-7
Theme: New life in Christ

Call to Worship

Pastor: God's grace and mercy has come alive in the birth of God's Son, Jesus our Savior.

People: Praise God for the birth of his Son!

Pastor: We enjoy a right relationship with God, not because of our righteousness, but because God has shared himself with us in the birth of his Son.

People: May the life we live reflect the joy we celebrate in the birth of our Savior.

Collect

Merciful God, you have shared your grace and mercy with us through the birth of your Son. Stir our hearts anew as we celebrate our Savior's birth; that we may learn to live a new life in reconciliation with you. In Christ's name we pray. Amen.

Prayer of Confession

You have given us new life, O God, in the birth of your Son. We celebrate his birth with joy, but quickly return to living the old life. Forgive us when we take only the celebration, and leave your grace and mercy unclaimed. Help us to experience the real Gift this Christmas, and live the new life which Jesus has brought to us. In his name we pray. Amen.

Hymns

"Hark! The Herald Angels Sing"
"It Came Upon the Midnight Clear"
"Love Came Down at Christmas"
"O Come, All Ye Faithful"

CHRISTMAS EVE/DAY
(Second Option)

Gospel: Luke 2:8-20
Theme: The Baby, a sign of salvation

Call to Worship
Pastor: Think again of that wonderful night when angels sang to shepherds.
People: It must have been a wonderful experience for them to see heaven unfold before their eyes.
Pastor: What the shepherds saw at the manger was only a sign of what was happening. It is still happening today.
People: Today we still experience the wonderful salvation that God has shared with us through his Son. How wonderful God is!

Collect
Almighty God, whose Son left his glory in heaven to share your glory with us: Draw us to the manger today, not to worship a baby, but to say "yes" to our Savior; that we may bring pleasure to you, and experience the peace Christ came to bring. In his name we pray. Amen.

Prayer of Confession
Lord, we have often come to the manger to see the Christ Child. But so many times we have not seen the sign of our salvation clearly enough to accept it. Forgive us for Christmases that are holidays instead of Holy Days. Save ys from sin as we open our hearts to your Son, our Savior, in whose name we pray. Amen.

Hymns
"Angels from the Realms of Glory"
"Silent Night, Holy Night"
"The First Noel"
"While Shepherd Watched Their Flocks"

CHRISTMAS EVE/DAY
(Third Option)

First Lesson: Isaiah 52:7-10
Theme: The announcement of salvation

Call To Worship

Pastor: Christ is born!
People: Christ is born indeed; salvation has come!
Pastor: Shout to our world the good news. God has brought peace to our world!
People: May our whole world see God's powerful love in the gift of his Son.

Collect

Merciful God, you have announced to our world the good news of salvation for all people. Help us to be faithful messengers of that good news; that our world may hear, and rejoice in the gift of your Son, Jesus, through whom we pray. Amen.

Prayer of Confession

Generation after generation, Lord, has heard the good news. We are blessed with peace, comfort, joy, and love. Yet generation after generation acts as if nothing has happened. Forgive our indifference which has kept us from hearing the real message of Christmas. Give us open ears and receptive hearts to the salvation which you have sent in your Son, Jesus. In his name we pray. Amen.

Hymns

"Away in a Manger"
"God Rest You Merry Gentlemen"
"There's a Song in the Air"
"What Child Is This?"

CHRISTMAS EVE/DAY
(Third Option)

Second Lesson: Hebrews 1:1-12
Theme: Christ's unique superiority

Call to Worship

Pastor: Come, celebrate the birth of Jesus, God's greatest revelation of himself.

People: Of all that God has done, Jesus most fully illustrates the true nature of God.

Pastor: We celebrate our Savior's birth, because through him, we are born into the glory of God.

People: Praise be to God for the birth of his Son! Praise be to Jesus for our rebirth into God's kingdom!

Collect

Glorious God, who has uncovered the glory of your kingdom in the birth of your Son: Help us to see in Jesus the hope of our rebirth; that we may begin anew to live the life you have created us to live. In Christ's name we pray. Amen.

Prayer of Confession

We praise your Son, O God, often because it is our ritual. But we want it to be because of our faith. Forgive us when we have sung praises with our lips which have not come from our hearts. Listen now to our hearts, and stir up within us true praise for the glorious gift of your Son, Jesus, our Savior. In his name we pray. Amen.

Hymns

"Angels from the Realms of Glory"
"Infant Holy, Infant Lowly"
"Love Came Down at Christmas"
"O God of Light, Thy Word, a Lamp"

CHRISTMAS EVE/DAY
(Third Option)

Gospel: John 1:1-14
Theme: God gives his people new birth

Call to Worship

Pastor: Jesus came into our world to give us knowledge of God, and to share God's gift of life, that we might become God's children.

People: Many people did not recognize Jesus as God's Son; and many still do not receive him as Lord.

Pastor: But all who do receive him, God adopts as his children who are reborn by his divine love.

People: We want to meet Jesus and begin a new life, reborn into God's family!

Collect

Almighty God, whose Word became flesh in Jesus your Son: May our hearts be receptive to him as Lord and Savior; that we may become your children, reborn by the power and love of your will. In our Savior's name we pray. Amen.

Prayer of Confession

O God of love, you have revealed yourself in the life of your Son, Jesus. He is our light, our life, and our hope. But we are of this world; and this world is indifferent to your gift of love. We are among those to whom your Son comes, who are prevented by sin from recognizing him as Savior. Forgive us for our sins that deny our sonship. Restore us to your fellowship; that we may enjoy the blessings of being your children. We pray through Christ our Lord. Amen.

Hymns

"At the Name of Jesus"
"I Know Not How That Bethlehem's Babe"
"O For a Thousand Tongues to Sing"
"Where Shall My Wondering Soul Begin"

FIRST SUNDAY AFTER CHRISTMAS

First Lesson: Isaiah 63:7-9
Theme: God gives his people mercy and love

Call to Worship

Pastor: God has called us to be his children, offering forgiveness through his Son, Jesus.

People: We are unworthy to be called his children, because through sin, we deny he is our Father.

Pastor: God has not forgotten his people. By grace, he reclaims us as his children.

People: God has made us his own through Christ! We are his people, and are called by his name.

Collect

O gracious Father, whose love and forgiveness is beyond measure: Fill our hearts to overflowing with joy and thanksgiving for your salvation; that all may see the blessings of those who take the name of Christ, our Lord and Savior, in whose name we pray. Amen.

Prayer of Confession

We are at the threshold of a new year, Father; and all we can offer you is lives marred by sin. Our past prevents us from offering you any record of righteousness. Forgive us for our sin which denies us the right to be called followers of Christ. Direct our attention to the future and your forgiveness, confident that you are leading your children into a new experience of Christian growth and commitment. We pray through Christ, our Lord and Savior. Amen.

Hymns

"God of the Ages, by Whose Hand"
"Take the Name of Jesus with You"
"There's a Wideness in God's Mercy"
" 'Tis So Sweet to Trust in Jesus"

FIRST SUNDAY AFTER CHRISTMAS

Second Lesson: Hebrews 2:10-18
Theme: Jesus leads us to salvation

Call to Worship

Pastor: Jesus has come to us from God, sharing our human nature in order to conquer that which destroys us.

People: Sin is the power that destroys us in death. We celebrate the presence of God who has come in the flesh, even Jesus our Savior.

Pastor: We receive God's forgiveness, because Jesus, who took on human form, intercedes on our behalf with God.

People: Because of Jesus, we are brought to God in a saving relationship. Praise the Lord for our salvation!

Collect

Heavenly Father, who has come to us in the birth of your Son to share our human nature for the sake of our salvation: Open our hearts to your presence as revealed in Jesus; that we may know the forgiveness which he imparts to us. In his name we pray. Amen.

Prayer of Confession

We are children of flesh, Father, but we desire to be born of the Spirit. We believe this is possible because Jesus intercedes on our behalf. Forgive us for our sins which lead us astray, denying that you are our Father. Increase our desire to follow Christ our Savior; that he may lead us to salvation. In his name we pray. Amen.

Hymns

"Blessed Assurance, Jesus Is Mine"
"I Know Not How That Bethlehem's Babe"
"Let All Together Praise Our God"
"Thou Hidden Source of Calm Repose"

FIRST SUNDAY AFTER CHRISTMAS

Gospel: Matthew 2:13-15, 19-23
Theme: God's protection of the infant Jesus

Call to Worship

Pastor: Even as an infant, Jesus was faced with rejection because of man's sinfulness.

People: King Herod felt threatened by Jesus' birth, and wanted to kill him.

Pastor: But God protected him by telling Joseph in a dream to take Jesus to Egypt.

People: Praise be to God for his divine protection of the infant Jesus!

Collect

Almighty God, whose divine providence enabled Jesus to perform his ministry to mankind: Remove any indifference on our part toward Jesus' ministry; that we may benefit by the salvation he brought to our world. In his name we pray. Amen.

Prayer of Confession

Forgive us, Father, for taking so much for granted in the Christian Faith. You have constantly had to pour out your love to people who seem bent on resisting that love. And we who want to accept your love, do so without considering the price you have paid. Sharpen our senses to see what wonderful feats you have performed in order that we might be redeemed from sin. In Jesus' name we pray. Amen.

Hymns

"Christ, Whose Glory Fills the Skies"
"Fairest Lord Jesus"
"Go Tell It on the Mountain"
"How Beauteous Were the Marks"

JANUARY 1
(When observed as New Year)

First Lesson: Deuteronomy 8:1-10
Theme: God's promise of providence

Call to Worship

Pastor: The future is exciting because it comes to us from God!

People: That's true. Fear of the unknown must give way to faith in God.

Pastor: God has promised to provide for our needs. Let us enter this new year with the assurance that God will take care of us.

People: We believe that for sure. We thank God for the new adventure we are ready to begin.

Collect
Benevolent God, you have called us to follow you with the promise that you will provide for our needs. Give us confidence in your promise as we begin this new year; that we may not falter in our faith from a fear of what we do not know. In the name of Christ we pray. Amen.

Prayer of Confession
Lord, we have been at the threshold of a new year many times; sometimes excited, sometimes afraid. We believe your promise to care for us, but fear is so powerful. Forgive our hesitancy, our doubts, and our fears when we focus on the unknown of tomorrow. Replace these handicaps with a bold assurance that this will be a year to rejoice because of your care for us. Hear us for Jesus' sake. Amen.

Hymns
"All the Way My Savior Leads Me"
"Be Not Dismayed"
"Forth in Thy Name"
"O God, Our Help in Ages Past"

JANUARY 1
(When observed as New Year)

Second Lesson: Revelation 21:1-6a
Theme: God's promise of his presence

Call to Worship

Pastor: God is the author of newness. He takes what is worn out, and replaces it with new.

People: This new year is like a preview of our new life in eternity. God will bless us with life that is totally new.

Pastor: The joy of God's newness is his presence, whether it is this new year we've never experienced before, or new life in eternity.

People: We praise God for his presence that makes every experience a new gift from him!

Collect

Eternal God, who promises to be with us in this new year, and through all eternity: Keep us mindful of your presence in all situations; that we may find strength and joy in whatever adventure you lead us. In the name of Christ we pray. Amen.

Prayer of Confession

You have given us many new years, Lord. But that which comes from you so new and pure, we quickly taint with sin. Forgive the new years we have made old by ignoring your presence. Walk with us each day; that we may now begin not just a new year, but a new life with you. In Jesus' name we pray. Amen.

Hymns

"O Come, and Dwell in Me"
"O Master, Let Me Walk with Thee"
" 'Tis So Sweet to Trust in Jesus"
"When We Walk with the Lord"

JANUARY 1
(When observed as New Year)

Gospel: Matthew 25:31-46
Theme: A new way to live

Call to Worship

Pastor: We have a new calendar, and a new year. It's a great time to begin a new life.

People: There is something reassuring about a new year. We can start over trying to live a better life.

Pastor: One of the best ways to live a better life is to live it for others. We serve Christ himself when we serve others.

People: May this new year be a new life in which we treat others as though Christ were present in them.

Collect

Almighty God, whose Son has challenged us to treat others with the same respect we would treat him: Keep us mindful of the service we may give to our Lord, by serving those in need; that both our world, and our Lord, may be blessed by our good deeds. In Christ's name we pray. Amen.

Prayer of Confession

We would do anything for your Son, O God, if he were here. He is, in the helpless, the homeless, and the hurt. But we turn our backs, thinking we have our eyes on Jesus. Forgive our unkindness to our brothers and sisters. Help us to see Jesus in those who cry for help; that our life might fulfill your will for those in need. In our Savior's name we pray. Amen.

Hymn

"Lord, Speak to Me"
"O Brother Man, Fold to Thy Heart"
"The Voice of God Is Calling"
"Where Cross the Crowded Ways"

SECOND SUNDAY AFTER CHRISTMAS

First Lesson: Jeremiah 31:7-14
Theme: Joy over God's salvation

Call to Worship

Pastor: Happy are those who have experienced Christ in Christmas!

People: Happy indeed, for Christ has brought us back into fellowship with God!

Pastor: Exiled by sin, restored by Christ: That is the good news Christmas proclaims.

People: The world will never be the same now that Christ has come. Praise God for our salvation!

Collect

O God of our salvation, you have dealt with our sin by sending your Son to be our Savior! How grateful we are for being restored in righteousness, not by any merit of ours, but by your Son. Keep us in the spirit of Christmas; that we may always remember his birth in our hearts is our source of true life. In Jesus' name we pray. Amen.

Prayer of Confession

How quickly Christmas is over, Lord. The carols, the decorations, and left over wrappings are stored away. And so is the joy that excited so many just a short time ago. Forgive our superficial Christmas, created by a secular society. Keep the song of the angels in our ears, and the joy of salvation in our hearts; that our Savior's birth may always excite us to love and serve you in thanksgiving for our salvation. In the name of Christ we pray. Amen.

Hymns

"Joy to the World"
"Joyful, Joyful We Adore Thee"
"Let All Together Praise Our God"
"O Little Town of Bethlehem"

SECOND SUNDAY AFTER CHRISTMAS

Second Lesson: Ephesians 1:3-6, 15-23
Theme: God gives his people new life

Call to Worship

Pastor: God, in his great love, chose us to be his children, and sent his Son to give us new life.

People: Without Christ, we are like homeless children, lost and wandering in a life of sin.

Pastor: It is God's plan for each of us to be a part of his family, and enjoy a new life blessed with his fatherly love.

People: Praise God for his grace and kindness which he has bestowed on us through Christ our Lord!

Collect

O loving Father, who desires to give your children new life through your Son, Jesus: Convince us to accept him as Lord and Savior; that we may enjoy new life as your children. In his name we pray. Amen.

Prayer of Confession

Father, we are your children only because you have poured out your love for us in your Son, Jesus. By nature we live the sinful life; and that has made it necessary for you to come to us with the patient and redeeming love of a father. Forgive us when we sin against your love, and refuse to live the new life you have given us through Christ. Increase our faith in your love; that we may rejoice in the new life that is ours. We pray in our Savior's name. Amen.

Hymns

"I Know Not How That Bethlehem's Babe"
"More Love to Thee, O Christ"
"O Jesus, I Have Promised"
"Take My Life, and Let It Be Consecrated"

SECOND SUNDAY AFTER CHRISTMAS

Gospel: John 1:1-18
Theme: God's word became flesh

Call to Worship

Pastor: The Word of God is not confined to the pages of our Bibles.

People: The Word of God is in our hearts as Christ reaffirms his birth in us.

Pastor: All who receive Jesus as God's Son become God's children, because that is his will.

People: We have experienced the glory of God in the birth of his Son. May we always live as children who are faithful to God's will.

Collect

Gracious God, you have come into our world with the gift of new life through your only Son. Grant us wills which coincide with your will; that we may be born anew in your kingdom, and live as those whom you are pleased to call your children. In the name of Christ we pray. Amen.

Prayer of Confession

We are your children, Father, but we confess there have been times when Christ has come to us, and we did not receive him. By your grace and mercy you did not desert us. Forgive our rejection; and hear the sincerity with which we claim Jesus as our Savior. Reveal your love to us through him as we study his life; that we may grow in our discipleship, giving you honor and glory. In our Savior's name we pray. Amen.

Hymns

"Father, in whom We Live"
"Love Divine, All Loves Excelling"
"O Word of God Incarnate"
"Spirit of God, Descend upon My Heart"

THE EPIPHANY
(January 6)

First Lesson: Isaiah 60:1-6
Theme: God's glory is seen as a light

Call to Worship

Pastor: We have seen God's glory revealed in his only . begotten Son, our Savior.

People: God's revelation in Christ is indeed a light that shines in our darkness.

Pastor: What a marvelous gift God has given to our world. Let us rejoice and sing his praises!

People: Our hearts thrill and rejoice as we come to worship our Lord!

Collect

Father of all nations: You have given yourself through your only begotten Son, as a radiant light revealing the path for all to follow who would be delivered from their darkness of sin. Let your light shine upon us; that we may share in the joy of knowing your Son as Lord and Savior. In his name we pray. Amen.

Prayer of Confession

We have celebrated your Son's birth, Father. And we have hailed him as our Savior. But we still need to make more of a response by walking in his light. Forgive us for saying wonderful things about him, without making the necessary changes in our lives which those wonderful things demand. Make our rejoicing a genuine response to his glory coming into our lives. We pray in his name. Amen.

Hymns

"Christ Is the World's True Light"
"Christ, Whose Glory Fills the Skies"
"Light of the World, We Hail Thee"
"Walk in the Light"

THE EPIPHANY
(January 6)

Second Lesson: Ephesians 3:1-12
Theme: Jews and Gentiles are one in Christ

Call to Worship

Pastor: God has revealed himself through Christ who is our Savior, and not ours only, but the Savior of the world.

People: In Christ we see that all mankind is one brotherhood, regardless of nationality.

Pastor: Being one in Christ means that all share in God's plan of salvation.

People: We praise God for his universal love and inclusive salvation.

Collect

W ful God, our Father, who has made all persons our br s and sisters in Christ: Correct our personal attn es which prevent us from being brothers and sisters to the rest of your Church; that we may truly be one, rejoicing harmoniously in our one Lord and Savior, even Jesus Christ, through whom we pray. Amen.

Prayer of Confession

We know, Father, that all mankind is one family. Your Son has revealed that to us. But we still are not as anxious to be one family as we ought to be. Forgive us for receiving our Lord's revelation as Lord and Savior, without accepting all others whom he came to save as our brothers and sisters. Guide us in strengthening the unity of your church by manifesting the Spirit of Christ in ourselves. We pray in his name. Amen.

Hymns

"Break Forth, O Living Light of God"
"Jesus, United by Thy Grace"
"One Holy Church of God Appears"
"The Church's One Foundation"

THE EPIPHANY
(January 6)

Gospel: Matthew 2:1-12
Theme: The visit of the wise men

Call to Worship

Pastor: We worship God our Father, whose glorious revelation in Christ was announced with wonderful signs.

People: The story of the wise men is the story of each of us in our search for God's special revelation.

Pastor: The star is bright enough even today for us to see the way to Christ, God's Savior of the world.

People: We have found our Savior as God promised; and we offer the best of ourselves in worship to him.

Collect

Almighty God: history records how even nature shared in proclaiming your wonderful revelation in Christ! Accept our worship as we bow before your Son in adoration. Then send us forth as messengers of your truth, that our whole world may know what you have done through Christ our Savior, in whose name we pray. Amen.

Prayer of Confession

You have spoken clearly through the beauty of nature in our world, Father. From distant lands persons came to bow in adoration of your Son. Forgive us for not lifting our eyes heavenward to see the star of your glory shining in our hearts today. Transform our churches into meeting places where we encounter your Son as our Savior; that we may share your glory with others. In our Savior's name we pray. Amen.

Hymns

"As with Gladness Men of Old"
"Brightest and Best"
"Earth Has Many a Noble City"
"We Three Kings"

BAPTISM OF OUR LORD
(First Sunday After the Epiphany)

First Lesson: Isaiah 42:1-9
Theme: God's Servant in whom he delights

Call to Worship

Pastor: God spoke through the prophet Isaiah describing his anointed servant with whom he was delighted.

People: When we think of Jesus' baptism, we cannot help thinking he was anointed to fulfill that prophecy.

Pastor: Jesus was certainly anointed with God's Spirit, and came as light to the nations.

People: He gives deliverance, freedom, and salvation. He is all that humanity needs, and all that God would want his anointed Servant to be. Praise his name!

Collect

O Lord God, our heavenly Father: Your promise of an anointed Servant has been fulfilled in Jesus. Grant that his ministry may so fulfill our needs; that we too, may delight in his healing work, and recognize him as your anointed one. Hear us for his sake. Amen.

Prayer of Confession

Father in heaven, we praise you for Jesus, your anointed Servant. But we confess it is too easy for us to speak of his servant role without letting him fulfill his ministry in us. Forgive us for the needs we have which we do not let Jesus minister to. Help us to learn how to let him be your servant to us and give us the healing and deliverance we need. In our Savior's name we pray. Amen.

Hymns

"All Hail the Power of Jesus' Name"
"Fairest Lord Jesus"
"Jesus, the Very Thought of Thee"
"O Son of God Incarnate"

BAPTISM OF OUR LORD
(First Sunday After the Epiphany)

Second Lesson: Acts 10:34-43
Theme: God's Spirit is present in Christ

Call to Worship

Pastor: Our Lord's ministry was blessed with God's saving presence to bring healing and wholeness.

People: Wherever Jesus went, God's power went with him ministering to those in need.

Pastor: Jesus' ministry continues today as he visits us with his saving presence.

People: We are people who need Jesus. We thank God he has ordained his Son to meet our needs, too.

Collect

Most merciful Father, who baptized your Son into a healing ministry which brings wholeness to body, mind, and soul: Give us the blessing of his saving presence, that we may experience healing which will restore us to wholeness. In our Savior's name we pray. Amen.

Prayer of Confession

We need so much of your saving presence, Father. But we become so passive when we publicly proclaim the power you have bestowed on Jesus. Forgive us for a witness that tells what he can do for others without showing how Jesus has first touched us. Reveal to us our brokenness; that salvation may be our rewarding experience with your Son, in whose name we pray. Amen.

Hymns

"At the Name of Jesus"
"Come, Thou Fount of Every Blessing"
"Jesus Is All the World to Me"
"O For a Thousand Tongues"

BAPTISM OF OUR LORD
(First Sunday After The Epiphany)

Gospel: Matthew 3:13-17
Theme: Jesus is baptized to be God's Servant

Call to Worship

Pastor: Jesus, who was sinless, accepted baptism by John in recognition of his willingness to be God's Servant.

People: His acceptance of God's will made him worthy to be God's anointed Servant.

Pastor: The Spirit of God came upon Jesus; and God announced to all that this was his Son with whom he was well pleased.

People: Praise be to Jesus, who accepted his calling to be God's Servant on our behalf!

Collect

Almighty God, who publicly announced at Jesus' baptism that he is your Son: Make us responsive to his mission as your Servant; that the work of your Spirit through him might bring us into reconciliation with you. We pray through Christ our Lord. Amen.

Prayer of Confession

We worship in adoration of your Son, O God. We hold him in high esteem, knowing you are pleased with his life and ministry. But we forget, Father, that you are pleased with him because of his willingness to minister to us. Forgive us when we have resisted that ministry. Send your Spirit to convict us of our sins, and convince us of your love in Christ to redeem us. In his name we pray. Amen.

Hymns

"All Praise to Thee, for Thou, O King Divine"
"Come, Every Soul by Sin Oppressed"
"Jesus, the Name High Over All"
"O Son of God Incarnate"

SECOND SUNDAY AFTER THE EPIPHANY

First Lesson: Isaiah 49:1-7
Theme: God's love is like that of a husband for his bride

Call To Worship

Pastor: When Jesus was anointed to be God's Servant, he was sent not as Savior of the Jews only.

People: His was a worldwide mission, that "salvation may reach to the end of the earth."

Pastor: Our Lord continues his mission through his church. We are to carry his message of salvation to all parts of the world.

People: We are servants of God's Servant. May we be faithful in telling our world the good news.

Collect

O God, our loving Father, who sent your Son into our world with a mission to bring all humanity into your salvation: Undergird your church to continue that mission in today's world; that none may be without the opportunity of hearing your word. We pray through Christ our Lord. Amen.

Prayer of Confession

We are your church, O God; and we have been called into being by your Son to carry out his mission of salvation to our world. Forgive us when we have failed in our responsibility, assuming someone else would carry our share of the load. Strengthen us in an effective ministry to our world; that we may convince others of salvation in Christ, in whose name we pray. Amen.

Hymns

"Go, Make of All Disciples"
"I Love to Tell the Story"
"O Zion, Haste"
"We've a Story to Tell"

SECOND SUNDAY AFTER THE EPIPHANY

Second Lesson: 1 Corinthians 1:1-9
Theme: The church is universal and united

Call to Worship

Pastor: We are God's church. And as his church we are united with all Christians everywhere.

People: To all who call upon the name of our Lord Jesus Christ: We are your brothers and sisters! The peace of Christ be with you all wherever you may be!

Pastor: Thanks be to God for his universal church united in Christ!

People: We are one in Christ's Spirit. Our love goes out in all directions as we join hearts around the world to worship our Lord.

Collect

Gracious Father, whose Son has called into being one church made up of all who believe in him as Lord and Savior: Unite us with all Christians in glad songs of praise as we express our gratitude for being members of Christ's body; that the spirit of unity may become a universal witness of all Christians. In our Savior's name we pray. Amen.

Prayer of Confession

We know the church is one, Father; but sometimes we look at our congregation and forget the whole church. Other times we do not want to recognize the whole body of Christ. Forgive us when discord, church doctrine, or prejudice hinders the unity of your church. Remind us of the source of our being, and our reason for being; that we may strive to make strong our witness in the world. We pray through Christ our Lord. Amen.

Hymns

"Blest Be the Tie That Binds"
"Happy the Souls to Jesus Joined"
"In Christ There Is No East or West"
"These Things Shall Be"

SECOND SUNDAY AFTER THE EPIPHANY

Gospel: John 1:29-41
Theme: Jesus is the Lamb of God

Call to Worship

Pastor: When Jesus assumed his servant role, he did more than just say what God wanted him to say.

People: He became the suffering servant whose suffering brings healing to others.

Pastor: In his suffering he took away the sins of the world which neither man nor the Law could do.

People: May God help us surrender to him, and lay all our sins at the foot of the cross.

Collect

Eternal God, who gave your only Son to suffer death on our behalf that we may be saved to new life: Draw us to you in humility and in penitence; that we may let Jesus take all our sins away and cleanse us from within. In his name we pray. Amen.

Prayer of Confession

We are sinful people who need your love, Father. You have expressed your love through your Son, Jesus, who offered himself as a sacrificial lamb in atonement for our sins. Forgive us for our wickedness that keeps us from being in a right relationship with you. Cleanse us by the blood of the Lamb, that we may walk in newness of life with Christ our Lord. In his name we pray. Amen.

Hymns

"Come, Ye Sinners, Poor and Needy"
"Have Thine Own Way, Lord"
"Jesus Is Tenderly Calling"
"O Happy Day"

50

THIRD SUNDAY AFTER THE EPIPHANY

First Lesson: Isaiah 9:1-4
Theme: Jesus' ministry brings light to those in darkness

Call to Worship

Pastor: Jesus began his ministry in Galilee as God's Servant, bringing light to those in darkness.

People: Isaiah had prophesied that Galilee would be filled with God's glory. That certainly came true in Jesus.

Pastor: Jesus' mission began in Galilee, but continues to reach out to all generations, sharing the light of God's love.

People: We have joy in our hearts because Christ's ministry has reached us. May our joy overflow and convey his love to others in our world.

Collect

Most merciful Father, whose Servant Son began a ministry which continues through your church today: Use us as servants of your Son, ministering to our world on his behalf, that your salvation may become known to our world. In the name of Christ we pray. Amen.

Prayer of Confession

We praise you O God, for your Son, who poured out his life in service that the light of his peace and joy may become realities for those in darkness. His mission has been entrusted to his church, and now we are to be in ministry. Forgive us for our immaturity which makes us want to be receivers of his light without being his messengers. May the testimony of our lives reflect the brightness of our Savior's love to the oppressed of our day. In his name we pray. Amen.

Hymns

"Go, Tell It on the Mountain"
"O God of Light, Thy Word, a Lamp"
"The People That in Darkness Sat"

THIRD SUNDAY AFTER THE EPIPHANY

Second Lesson: 1 Corinthians 1:10-17
Theme: A call for harmony in the church

Call to Worship

Pastor: The church belongs to Christ; and therefore ought to be united in one harmonious witness.

People: We know we are Christ's people; but our human nature often interferes. And what ought to be harmony becomes discord.

Pastor: When divisions arise, we need to remind ourselves our differences are various parts of Christ's one church, and pledge our allegiance to him.

People: May God help us grow into a mature understanding of the unity of Christ's church.

Collect

Almighty Father, who has brought your children into one church through the sacrificial ministry of your Son: Heal the fractures which hurt your church today, that harmony may add strength to the faith we proclaim to our world. In the name of Christ we pray. Amen.

Prayer of Confession

We cannot really point a finger at the Corinthian Church, Father. We have our divisions, too. And they hurt the outreach of your church today. Forgive us for our self-interests which compete with the unity of your church. Restore a singleness of heart to your church, that Christ's death on the cross may not be robbed of its power. In our Savior's name we pray. Amen.

Hymns

"All Praise to Our Redeeming Lord"
"Blest Be the Dear Uniting Love"
"Father, We Thank Thee Who Hast Planted"
"We Are One in the Spirit"

52

THIRD SUNDAY AFTER THE EPIPHANY

Gospel: Matthew 4:12-23
Theme: Called to be in mission

Call to Worship
Pastor: Jesus began his ministry by calling disciples to follow him and be in mission for him.
People: Jesus is still calling disciples to carry out his mission in the world.
Pastor: Our mission is an all inclusive mission to share Christ with our world.
People: We have good news to tell! We pray that we will miss no one as we share Christ's message.

Collect
Most holy God, whose Son began a ministry with disciples, and continues that ministry today with responsive followers: Make us quick to give of ourselves to be in mission as your church today, that the good news of Christ may bring wholeness in all parts of our world. In Jesus' name we pray. Amen.

Prayer of Confession
We love your church, O God, and are glad to be a part of it. But we fail so often to be in mission. Too many people are not receiving the ministry of your church because of our reluctance. Forgive us for our poor discipleship. Revive us with renewed concern for the lost in the world, that we may join hands as one church with new fervor to share Christ with our world. In his name we pray. Amen.

Hymns
"Christ for the World We Sing"
"Heralds of Christ"
"Jesus Calls Us"
"O Zion, Haste"

FOURTH SUNDAY AFTER THE EPIPHANY

First Lesson: Micah 6:1-8
Theme: The righteousness God requires

Call to Worship

Pastor: As we begin our worship this morning, reflect on the wonderful ways God has proved his love to you.

People: God has blessed us with guidance, comfort, strength, love, and forgiveness. God has been very good to us!

Pastor: God has saved us to live a new life; a life of righteousness, love, and fellowship with him.

People: May the worship we give to God be this kind of life, lived in thanksgiving for our salvation.

Collect

Gracious God, you have demonstrated your love in so many ways to accomplish our salvation. Make clear our memory of your kindness to us; that we may respond by living in accordance with your will, without any false appearance of sincerity. In the name of Christ we pray. Amen.

Prayer of Confession

We can worship by ritual, Lord, but many times our heart is not in it. It becomes a mask, and we are poor actors. Forgive us when the life we live contradicts the worship we would portray in your house. Help us to live the righteous life you have saved us to live, so that the ritual we follow will be an honest witness of the worship we live. In our Savior's name we pray. Amen.

Hymns

"I Want a Principle Within"
"O For A Thousand Tongues to Sing"
"O Worship the King"
"Take My Life and Let It Be Consecrated"

FOURTH SUNDAY AFTER THE EPIPHANY

Second Lesson: 1 Corinthians 1:18-31
Theme: Boast only in what the Lord has done

Call to Worship

Pastor: We are not Christians very long until we are tempted to keep track of our good deeds.

People: We cannot help wanting to make ourselves feel we have earned at least a little of God's love.

Pastor: Yes, but that breeds sin. None of us, whether by intelligence, or by devotion, can boast of what we offer to our Lord.

People: God forgive us, and help us to boast only of what he has done for us!

Collect

God of all wisdom, who confuses the wise and the strong with the simplicity of faith: Interpret discipleship to us; that we may not boast of any wisdom or strength of our own as means of accomplishing righteousness, but trust only in your mercy and grace. We pray in Jesus' name. Amen.

Prayer of Confession

We forget too quickly, Father, just where we were when you called us into the Christian Faith. None of us has been called on the basis of our righteousness, or our wisdom, or our power. We were called on the basis of our need of your forgiveness. Forgive us when we let ourselves think that our good works have brought us into your favor. Reveal to us that any righteousness of ours is due only to what you have done for us in Christ Jesus our Lord, through whom we pray. Amen.

Hymns

"Amazing Grace"
"Jesus, My Strength, My Hope"
"O Could I Speak the Matchless Worth"
"Praise, My Soul, the King of Heaven"

FOURTH SUNDAY AFTER THE EPIPHANY

Gospel: Matthew 5:1-12
Theme: The Beatitudes

Call to Worship

Pastor: One of our greatest goals in life is to find happiness.

People: We do not enjoy being unhappy. But the more we strive for happiness, the less we seem to have.

Pastor: Perhaps our attempts to be happy, work against what our Lord does to make us happy.

People: Our concept of happiness needs to be redesigned by our faith. May God give us the joy of true happiness.

Collect

Merciful Father, whose fatherly goodness makes happy those who put their trust in you: Cause us to see who we are as your children; that we may experience the happiness you have said is ours. We pray through Jesus Christ our Lord. Amen.

Prayer of Confession

Life is full of joy, Father, but too often we make ourselves satisfied with that which is only superficial happiness. Forgive us for spending life in a struggle to be happy when true happiness can be ours by putting our trust in you. Grant us the blessings that belong to those who gladly live as your children, that joy may become our true nature. In our Savior's name we pray. Amen.

Hymns

"Blest Are the Pure in Heart"
"God, Who Touchest Earth with Beauty"
"Happiness Is to Know the Savior"
"Happy the Souls to Jesus Joined"

FIFTH SUNDAY AFTER THE EPIPHANY

First Lesson: Isaiah 58:3-9a
Theme: True worship is sharing with the needy

Call to Worship

Pastor: We worship God by giving ourselves in devotion to him.

People: We have many forms of worship; but it is too easy to sit through these forms without giving ourselves to God.

Pastor: That is why God asks for true worship to be expressed in the form of sharing this world's goods with the needy.

People: May the worship we profess in the sanctuary find expression in genuine concern for the poor and hungry.

Collect

Almighty God, who requires worship to reach beyond ritual into the area of benevolent service: Inspire in us honest devotion which will motivate genuine love for those less fortunate, that we may enjoy the blessing of your guiding presence in our lives. We pray through Christ our Lord. Amen.

Prayer of Confession

We have expressed our worship in too small a place, Father, and the real sanctuary of our world is desecrated by our unwillingness to share with our brothers. Forgive us for the empty expressions we have offered as worship, while failing to express our love by reaching out to others in need. Lead us by your Spirit in true worship, that we may feel our brothers' need, and minister to that need. In our Savior's name we pray. Amen.

Hymns

"O Brother Man, Fold to Thy Heart"
"The Voice of God Is Calling"
"We Thank Thee, Lord"
"Where Cross the Crowded Ways of Life"

FIFTH SUNDAY AFTER THE EPIPHANY

Second Lesson: 1 Corinthians 2:1-11
Theme: God is the power of the gospel, not man

Call to Worship

Pastor: The greatness of the gospel is not determined by the persons who proclaim it.

People: The gospel is great because it is God's revelation of his love and power.

Pastor: We need dedicated leaders to help us grow in the faith; but the real basis of faith is the presence of God in our lives.

People: We ask God to help us stand firm in the faith, trusting in his power to redeem us.

Collect

Heavenly Father, whose very being is the gospel which thrills our hearts: Confirm our faith in you, that we may not let the frailities of human wisdom weaken our commitment to you. We pray in Jesus' name. Amen.

Prayer of Confession

We know the gospel is your word, Father, and not man's. But we are prone to react to the gospel with indifference when we see undesirable qualities in those who proclaim it. Forgive us for our pettiness which prevents us from standing firm in the Christian Faith, with conviction to live committed lives. Add strength to our faith by the power of your Spirit as we witness to one another. In our Savior's name we pray. Amen.

Hymns

"Author of Faith, Eternal Word"
"How Firm a Foundation"
"How Great Thou Art"
"O For a Faith that Will Not Shrink"

FIFTH SUNDAY AFTER THE EPIPHANY

Gospel: Matthew 5:13-16
Theme: Engaged in self-giving ministry

Call to Worship

Pastor: Christ has called his church into being to share his message of salvation with our world.

People: The church has brought God's love to us; now we are commissioned to share his love with others.

Pastor: Jesus used the illustrations of salt and light to show we have a caring and sharing ministry.

People: We are in Christ's ministry. May God help us to be effective in that ministry.

Collect

Almighty God, who challenges your church with a ministry which lightens and enhances the lives of others: Lead us into committed service, that our ministry may bring wholeness to our world through Christ our Lord, in whose name we pray. Amen.

Prayer of Confession

We believe the church has the best message our world could hear, Father. But we become silent so easily; and we are like salt which has lost its taste, or a light that has grown dim. Forgive us for our lack of genuine concern and enthusiasm to give ourselves in ministry to our world. Refresh us by your Spirit, that we may accept your challenge and win others into your kingdom. In our Savior's name we pray. Amen.

Hymns

"Brightly Beams Our Father's Mercy"
"Forth in Thy Name"
"O Thou Who Camest from Above"
"Rescue the Perishing"

SIXTH SUNDAY AFTER THE EPIPHANY

First Lesson: Deuteronomy 30:15-20
Theme: Choose God and live

Call to Worship

Pastor: God has created life in such a way, that evil cannot give the blessings which God gives to those who follow him.

People: Those who follow the commandments of God are blessed with joy and happiness now and forever.

Pastor: But the choice is ours whether we follow evil and perish, or choose God and live.

People: We choose God. May we witness to that fact by our love, our obedience, and our discipleship.

Collect

Almighty God, who has set before us the choice of good or evil, with the promise of life or death: Convince us of your love, and of our need of your love, that we may not turn our hearts from you and perish in our sins. We pray in Jesus' name. Amen.

Prayer of Confession

We have made our choice to follow you, Father. But we forget that every day we must choose. Too often, our negligence to choose righteousness leads us into the way of sin. Forgive us for our failure to consciously decide each day to live in accordance with your will. Convict us of our sins, and share with us your forgiveness, that we may remain in fellowship with you. We pray through Christ our Lord. Amen.

Hymns

"Have Thine Own Way, Lord"
"O Happy Day, That Fixed My Choice"
"Take My Life, and Let It Be Consecrated"
"When We Walk with the Lord"

SIXTH SUNDAY AFTER THE EPIPHANY

Second Lesson: 1 Corinthians 3:1-9
Theme: Partners serving God

Call to Worship

Pastor: Christian service requires many different kinds of servants.

People: The service of each is vitally important to the work that God is doing for all people.

Pastor: We are partners with each other and with God. God needs each of us to work together, so that he will be able to do his work.

People: May the service we give be in cooperation, not competition, with other servants working with God.

Collect

Almighty God, who has called us to be partners in the service of your Son: Put a spirit of unity and cooperation in your church; that together we serve in a variety of ways to interpret your message of redemption to our world. In our Savior's name we pray. Amen.

Prayer of Confession

We know you need many different kinds of servants, Lord. But we tend to regard different acts of service on different levels of importance. Forgive us when jealousy or misunderstanding causes us to quarrel in the administration of your church. May our motivation for service be love; that we may give our best, knowing that it is only your act of love that brings about salvation. In Christ's name we pray. Amen.

Hymns

"All Praise to Our Redeeming Love"
"Jesus, United by Thy Grace"
"Lift Up Our Hearts, O King of Kings"
"The Voice of God Is Calling"

SIXTH SUNDAY AFTER THE EPIPHANY

Gospel: Matthew 5:17-26
Theme: Righteousness fulfills the law

Call to Worship

Pastor: By grace we are saved. But God's grace is not contrary to his law.

People: To be saved by grace does not mean we do not have to live by God's law.

Pastor: Jesus came to save us apart from the law, but also to challenge us to live by love, a life that fulfills the law.

People: May the grace of God so motivate us that our living will demonstrate obedience to God's law.

Collect

Gracious God, you have saved us by grace in spite of our disobedience to your will; that our lives may become an offering of thanksgiving for your grace. In Jesus' name we pray. Amen.

Prayer of Confession

We pride ourselves, Lord, on being children of grace instead of slaves of the law. But often our lives do not reflect the wholeness to which you have saved us. Forgive us when we think only of your grace, and ignore our discipleship. Help us to choose to live in such a way that our life style will be in harmony with your will for us. In our Savior's name we pray. Amen.

Hymns

"God, Send Us Men"
"Lord, I Want to Be a Christian"
"Take Time to Be Holy"
"When We Walk With The Lord"

SEVENTH SUNDAY AFTER THE EPIPHANY

First Lesson: Isaiah 49:8-13
Theme: God does not forget his people

Call to Worship

Pastor: God has promised us that he will never leave us,
or forget that he is our God.

**People: Even when we think God has deserted us, he is
present to give us hope and encouragement.**

Pastor: God keeps his promises. It is up to us to believe
and trust him.

**People: Our faith is strengthened as we put our trust in
God. We know he will be faithful to us.**

Collect

Gracious Father, whose faithfulness to your children never
wavers: Transform our fears and doubts into confidence in
your guiding presence, that we may be filled with the joy
of salvation. We pray in our Savior's name. Amen.

Prayer of Confession

Life is full of difficulties, Father; and often our inability to
endure makes us feel you are not present to undergird us.
Forgive us when we have given in to defeat so quickly,
instead of putting our trust in you for your guidance. Make
your presence felt in our hearts, and in our lives; that we
may never feel you are far from us, or unconcerned about
our needs. We pray through Jesus Christ our Lord. Amen.

Hymns

"God of Our Life"
"Great Is Thy Faithfulness"
"How Firm a Foundation"
"If Thou But Suffer God to Guide Thee"

SEVENTH SUNDAY AFTER THE EPIPHANY

Second Lesson: 1 Corinthians 3:10-11, 16-23
Theme: Jesus is the foundation of the church

Call to Worship

Pastor: The church has weathered many storms, but it survives because Jesus is the sure foundation.

People: Human nature in the church makes it subject to all kinds of disagreements which hurt the unity of the church.

Pastor: The faith of the church is in Christ, not in the doctrines and dogmas designed by man.

People: Many persons have done great things in the church. But we know Christ is the real source of our being. Praise his name!

Collect

Gracious Father, whose Son is the only foundation on which the church is built: Use the labors of consecrated Christians to lead us to Christ; that trusting him, we may be defended against the threats which human nature brings into the church. In Christ's name we pray. Amen.

Prayer of Confession

Persons can be very persuasive, Father; and we respond on the basis of their interpretation of the gospel. But this causes us to take our eyes off Jesus, and we see the church more in human dimensions than divine. Forgive us for commitments we have made which have contributed to fractures, rather than to growth in the church. Set us straight in our faith; that we may be firmly rooted in Christ Jesus our Lord, through whom we pray. Amen.

Hymns

"Christ Is Made the Sure Foundation"
"My Hope Is Built"
"One Holy Church of God Appears"
"The Church's One Foundation"

SEVENTH SUNDAY AFTER THE EPIPHANY

Gospel: Matthew 5:27-37
Theme: Sin begins with inner motives

Call to Worship

Pastor: Jesus taught that sin begins with our inner motives where the Law is unable to give direction.

People: God knows the secrets of our hearts; and he desires that we surrender our wills to him.

Pastor: Our relationship with God is determined by how we feel in our hearts. That is where we must get right with God if we are to be true to him.

People: We justify ourselves by the laws we have kept. But we know we need God to cleanse our hearts.

Collect

Almighty God, whose son has exposed the secret hiding place of our sins: Cleanse us from within; that our hearts may belong to you, allowing us to live in complete surrender to your will. In our Savior's name we pray. Amen.

Prayer of Confession

We realize laws are important, Father. But we also know how we manipulate laws so that we can still satisfy our wills. Forgive us for our inner motives which are contrary to your will. Transform our lives by your indwelling Spirit; and lead us into righteous living. We pray in the name of Christ our Lord. Amen.

Hymns

"Come, Thou Fount"
"Draw Thou My Soul, O Christ"
"Take My Life, and Let It Be Consecrated"
"Truehearted, Wholehearted"

EIGHTH SUNDAY AFTER THE EPIPHANY

First Lesson: Leviticus 19:1-2, 9-18
Theme: Love your neighbor as yourself

Call to Worship

Pastor: We are the children of God; and as his children we are to love one another.

People: We deny God as our Father when we are unkind or unfair to each other.

Pastor: Therefore we are commanded by God to love our neighbors as ourselves.

People: May our attitude in society prove we are children of God.

Collect

Gracious Father, whose nature to love is a basic requirement for those who would be your children: Empty our hearts of bitterness, jealousy, and vengeance; that we may give to society the example of brotherly love. In our Savior's name we pray. Amen.

Prayer of Confession

We need people to be our neighbors, Father. But we are guilty of many unneighborly acts of injustice; and we carelessly violate their right to depend on us as neighbors. Forgive us for pretending to love when we use people to our advantage, and then mistreat them when they displease us. Give us the desire to express genuine love and concern for one another as you have commanded. We pray in Jesus' name. Amen.

Hymns

"At Length There Dawns the Glorious Day"
"O Brother Man, Fold to Thy Heart"
"These Things Shall Be"
"Where Cross the Crowded Ways of Life"

EIGHTH SUNDAY AFTER THE EPIPHANY

Second Lesson: 1 Corinthians 4:1-5
Theme: Our faith does not make us judge of others

Call to Worship

Pastor: When we surrender our lives to Christ, the assurance of salvation fills us with joy.

People: It is the most wonderful experience! We wish everyone could enjoy it.

Pastor: Christ gives himself in different ways to different people, and therefore cautions us not to judge the Christian experience of others.

People: There is one Christ, one church. May our experience with Christ preserve that unity.

Collect

O Holy God, whose church is made of many different personalities who have had different experiences with Christ: Give us understanding hearts; that we may work in harmony, instead of judging the Christian witness of others. In Jesus' name we pray. Amen.

Prayer of Confession

We enjoy Christian fellowship, Father; but we are too biased as to whom we include in our fellowship. We become critical of some who call themselves Christians, who do not seem to be true to the faith according to our experience. Forgive us for our judgmental attitude toward them. Help us to fellowship in Christian love with them, leaving all judgment in the hands of Christ, through whom we pray. Amen.

Hymns

"Christ Is Made the Sure Foundation"
"O Church of God, United"
"O Day of God, Draw Nigh"
"The Church's One Foundation"

EIGHTH SUNDAY AFTER THE EPIPHANY

Gospel: Matthew 5:38-48
Theme: Love your enemies

Call to Worship

Pastor: Jesus added to the teaching of the Old Testament, saying we must love not only our friends, but even our enemies.

People: Many people who are not Christians love their friends; but Jesus expects us to go farther than that in giving our love.

Pastor: That is the way God loves us. He wants his children to love in the same way.

People: May God help us to be more loving toward those who do not love us.

Collect

O loving Father, who has demonstrated your love in Christ, and has instructed us to love even our enemies: Melt the hardness of our hearts which keeps us from loving those who do not love us; that we may truly become your children. In our Savior's name we pray. Amen.

Prayer of Confession

We follow the way of the world so easily, Father. And our circle of friends grows smaller. Forgive us when we have not reached out in love to all persons, even those who would be our enemies. Help us better to understand your love for us, that we may become more free in sharing our love with others. We pray in the name of Christ our Lord. Amen.

Hymns

"Christ for the World We Sing"
"Lift Up Our Hearts, O King of Kings"
"O Young and Fearless Prophet"
"Rise Up, O Men of God"

TRANSFIGURATION
(Last Sunday After the Epiphany)

First Lesson: Exodus 24:12-18
Theme: Moses experiences the glory of the Lord

Call to Worship

Pastor: At times we are privileged to have "mountaintop" experiences with our Lord.

People: The glory of God is so real as he comes to us, and blesses us.

Pastor: God is a glorious God. Even though we cannot stay on the mountain, we are always in his presence.

People: Blessing and honor be to God who wonderfully makes himself known to us!

Collect

Most glorious Father, who in wondrous ways has given your glory to mankind: Let the light of your glory flood our lives with your presence, that we may be lifted up by the power of your Spirit to live faithful lives. We pray in the name of Christ our Lord. Amen.

Prayer of Confession

We know about your glory, Father; but too often it is second-hand information instead of our own experience. Forgive us when we have stayed at the foot of the mountain when you would have lifted us up into your presence. Revive us with the wonder of your glory; that we may be inspired by your holiness, and challenged to deeper commitment. Hear us for Jesus' sake. Amen.

Hymns

"Holy, Holy, Holy! Lord God Almighty"
"O Splendor of God's Glory Bright"
"O Worship the King"
"The Lord Jehovah Reigns"

TRANSFIGURATION
(Last Sunday After the Epiphany)

Second Lesson: 2 Peter 1:16-21
Theme: The experience of Christ's glory

Call to Worship

Pastor: We love to tell the stories of Jesus because we know they are true.

People: We learn much about Jesus from the stories in the Bible. But those stories mean even more to us because we see ourselves in many of those stories.

Pastor: Our greatest understanding of Jesus comes from our personal experiences with him. Scripture and experience produce a living faith.

People: With our own hearts, we have experienced our Savior's love and praise him for saving us!

Collect

Almighty God, who has revealed the glory of your Son to Christians of every generation: Open our hearts to the blessed experience of his glory and our lips to the saving message of his love; that his coming to earth so long ago may redeem lives even today. In his name we pray. Amen.

Prayer of Confession

So often, Father, we stumble in darkness when you have given us the light of the world. Forgive us when we hide in the shadows of shallow faith, instead of rejoicing in the glory of Christ's redemption. Grant us the joy of Christ making his presence known to us. In his name we pray. Amen.

Hymns

"God of All Power and Truth and Grace"
"Jesus, Thine All-Victorious Love"
"Love Divine, All Loves Excelling"
"O Come, and Dwell in Me"

TRANSFIGURATION
(Last Sunday After the Epiphany)

Gospel: Matthew 17:1-9
Theme: Jesus' transfiguration

Call to Worship

Pastor: The glory of Christ was revealed in his transfiguration as witnessed by Peter, James, and John.

People: Jesus is truly human and divine, the Son of God who has come to humanity!

Pastor: We see Jesus not only as a historical person of the past, but as living Lord in every generation.

People: Glory be to God the Father, who shares his divine nature through his ever-present Son!

Collect

Holy God our heavenly Father, who has revealed your Son to us as divine Lord: Open our eyes to see his glory, that we may give our devotion to him through committed living. In his name we pray. Amen.

Prayer of Confession

We are always in the presence of your divine Son, O God; but we are not always aware of his glory. Our familiarity with faith sometimes causes us to be careless in our devotion. Forgive us when we have been blind to your divine revelation in Christ. Light a fire of devotion in our hearts which will burn throughout our lives, giving us the warmth of his presence. In our Savior's name we pray. Amen.

Hymns

"Crown Him with Many Crowns"
"Jesus! the Name High over All"
"Joyful, Joyful, We Adore Thee"
"We Would See Jesus"

ASH WEDNESDAY

First Lesson: Joel 2:1-2,12-17a
Theme: A call to repentance

Call to Worship

Pastor: We stand before a very holy God who calls us into a life of holiness.

People: But we are unholy. Even our religious ceremonies do not cleanse us of our sins.

Pastor: God wants us to be truly penitent in our hearts, more than he wants our religious ceremonies. Then he will cleanse us of our sins.

People: May our worship be an honest expression of repentance and returning to God.

Collect

Holy Father, who is grieved by our sinfulness, and yet still offers forgiveness to the penitent: Hear the cries of our hearts as we repent of our sins, that your forgiveness may restore us in fellowship with you. We pray through Christ our Lord. Amen.

Prayer of Confession

We are religious people, Father, otherwise we would not be here on this special day. But much of our religion is expressed in ritual rather than in righteousness. Forgive us for our sinfulness, and for our pious ways of ignoring our sins. Keep our hearts in tune with you, that we may always be in the spirit of true repentance. In our Savior's name we pray. Amen.

Hymns

"Have Thine Own Way, Lord"
"Just As I Am, Without One Plea"
"More Love to Thee, O Christ"
"Out of the Depths I Cry to Thee"

ASH WEDNESDAY

Second Lesson: 2 Corinthians 5:20b—6:2 (3-10)
Theme: Be reconciled to God

Call to Worship

Pastor: Hear Paul's plea to the church: Be reconciled to God on behalf of Christ.

People: God's grace has come to us in Christ. We do not want it to be wasted.

Pastor: Then let us give our lives to Christ, who took on himself our sins, that we may be forgiven.

People: The day of salvation is here! We commit ourselves to Christ as our Lord and Savior.

Collect

Gracious Father, who made your Son share our sin that we may share your righteousness: Make today a day of salvation in which we are reconciled to you by the grace of your Son Jesus Christ, in whose name we pray. Amen.

Prayer of Confession

Forgive us, Father, for our sins which separate us from you, making us your enemies. Let your Son be our Savior; that by his grace we can be made your friends, and enjoy your gift of salvation. Strengthen us in our discipleship to remain firm in our faith, and loyal in our service. We pray through Christ our Lord. Amen.

Hymns

"Amazing Grace"
"Come, Every Soul by Sin Oppressed"
"I Am Coming to the Cross"
"I Gave My Life for Thee"

ASH WEDNESDAY

Gospel: Matthew 6:1-6, 16-21
Theme: Practice piety in secret

Call to Worship

Pastor: The Christian life is a disciplined life of devotion to God, and service to our fellow man.

People: But we must be careful that our devotion and service do not become public expressions of piety.

Pastor: Our piety is something between ourselves and God. The praise of man is not a goal of Christian living.

People: May our discipleship be a source of joy to God, without appearing as pretensions of self-righteous behavior.

Collect

Almighty God, who blesses those who give themselves to you in devotion: Guide us in our discipleship; that we may not submit to the glory of public piety, but give ourselves and our service as true reverence to you. In Jesus' name we pray. Amen.

Prayer of Confession

We have difficulty, Father, in wanting to be righteous without appearing as self-righteous. We often fail in discipleship because of not wanting to practice our piety before others. Then, too, we have been pleased with the praise of others for our righteousness. Forgive us for our humanness which hinders our expression of devotion to you. Help us give ourselves in holiness with no other concern than to please you. We pray through Christ our Lord. Amen.

Hymns

"Be Thou My Vision"
"Forth in Thy Name"

FIRST SUNDAY IN LENT

First Lesson: Genesis 2:4b-9, 15-17, 25—3:7
Theme: We are sinners by our own choice

Call to Worship

Pastor: We have each been to the garden, and have eaten freely of the forbidden tree in spite of God's commands.

People: We seem unable to help ourselves when it comes to resisting temptation.

Pastor: That is because we share the human nature of Adam. We know God's laws, but we choose sin.

People: We come guilty of sin, asking God to reclaim us as his children.

Collect

Almighty God, whose wondrous creation we have defied by our willful sinning: Cause us to see clearly our identity with the sinfulness of Adam; that we may accept full responsibility for our guilt, and come to you, seeking forgiveness and renewed fellowship through Christ our Savior. Amen.

Prayer of Confession

We see too much of Adam in ourselves, Father; and we tend to blame you for creating us that way. Forgive us for our many sins, and for our unwillingness to accept responsibility for our sinful behavior. Convince us of your love, sinful as we are; that we may give more devotion to your divine laws, and less allegiance to our sinful nature. Hear us for Christ's sake. Amen.

Hymns

"How Can a Sinner Know"
"Jesus, the Sinner's Friend"
"Sing Them Over Again to Me"
"Sinners, Turn: Why Will You Die"

FIRST SUNDAY IN LENT

Second Lesson: Romans 5:12-19
Theme: Christ, the second Adam

Call to Worship

Pastor: It is not difficult to know what Adam was like even though he lived so long ago.

People: We act just like him today, as though his sinfulness somehow makes us sinners.

Pastor: We do share Adam's nature. But more important is the fact that Christ has come; and through him, redemption can be ours.

People: Our trust is in Christ, who transforms our sinful nature into wholeness by the redemptive forgiveness of God's love for his children!

Collect

O Loving Father, whose divine nature has come to man in the gift of your Son, redeeming our sinful nature: Clothe us with the nature of Christ; that we may grow in his likeness, and discard our likeness to Adam. In our Savior's name we pray. Amen.

Prayer of Confession

There is a struggle within us, Father, and we need your help. We sin so easily with the nature of Adam; but we are not happy as sinners. Forgive us for our likeness to Adam, and remake us in your image as revealed in Christ. Make us free from our sins as we submit to the guidance of your Son, our Savior, in whose name we pray. Amen.

Hymns

"Come, Thou Fount of Every Blessing"
"Jesus Is All the World to Me"
"O For a Thousand Tongues"
"O Sacred Head, Now Wounded"

FIRST SUNDAY IN LENT

Gospel: Matthew 4:1-11
Theme: Jesus' temptation

Call to Worship

Pastor: Jesus revealed his uniqueness in being fully human and divine when he was tempted.

People: He came to us from God, and yet to be one of us, he had to face our temptations.

Pastor: He overcame those temptations, and through his victory he stands as one in whom we can put our trust.

People: May Christ's power over temptation become the redemptive power through which he transforms our lives.

Collect

Eternal God: You have sent your Son whose faithfulness to you gave him victory over the power of temptation. May our hearts be submissive to him, that his victory may become ours, and our wills may become yours. We pray through Christ our Lord. Amen.

Prayer of Confession

We have learned to accept temptation's power without feeling a sense of guilt, Father. It surrounds us like the atmosphere, and we let it become the breath that sustains our life. But such life does not grow, and we feel close to death. Forgive us for our ignorance of the truth of temptation's power to kill, and for not expereincing victory over temptation through Christ. In his name we pray. Amen.

Hymns

"Go to Dark Gethsemane"
"He Who Would Valiant Be"
"O Come, and Dwell in Me"
"Take the Name of Jesus with You"

SECOND SUNDAY IN LENT

First Lesson: Genesis 12:1-4a (4b-8)
Theme: God's call of Abraham

Call to Worship

Pastor: God has done mighty things in history because people have responded to his call.

People: We remember Abraham and the promise God made to him with the call to go to a new land.

Pastor: God still calls people to participate in his salvation by following his directions.

People: We believe God is calling us. We pray he will help us to hear, and follow.

Collect

Heavenly Father, who calls people of every generation to share in your salvation: Speak clearly to us, and give us responsive hearts; that we may find the happiness of obedient living promised to those who hear and follow your son, through whom we pray. Amen.

Prayer of Confession

We drift from one day to the next, Father, with no real purpose in being alive. Yet we long for life, and dream of better days which we call tomorrow. Forgive us for detaining that tomorrow by not listening to your voice which calls us to live our days with you. Open our ears and our hearts; that, as we hear your call, you may be able to work a mighty work in your church today. In our Savior's name we pray. Amen.

Hymns

"God Calling Yet"
"I Am Thine, O Lord"
"Jesus Calls Us O'er the Tumult"
"O Jesus, I Have Promised"

SECOND SUNDAY IN LENT

Second Lesson: Romans 4:1-5 (6-12) 13-17
Theme: Faith comes before good works

Call to Worship

Pastor: We believe behavior is important; and so we stress good works.

People: But before good works are really good, there must first be faith.

Pastor: Yes! It was because of Abraham's faith, not his works, that God considered him righteous.

People: We want to do good; but we want our goodness to be an honest expression of our faith in God.

Collect

Gracious Father, who challenges us to trust completely in your redemption: Remove from us all that encourages doubt or shallow belief; that with full confidence in your divine love, we may follow your will, believing sincerely that we have salvation in Christ Jesus your Son, through whom we pray. Amen.

Prayer of Confession

We want to do good, Father; but too often we find ourselves doing that which is not good. We fail because our faith fails; and we cannot keep doing good just for the sake of doing good. Forgive us for our disinterest or doubts which keep us from knowing and believing you. Cause our faith to mature; that we may commit ourselves to sincere discipleship. In Jesus' name we pray. Amen.

Hymns

"All the Way My Savior Leads Me"
"God of the Ages, by Whose Hand"
"My Faith Looks Up to Thee"
"O For a Faith that Will Not Shrink"

SECOND SUNDAY IN LENT

Gospel: John 3:1-17
Theme: Jesus' invitation to drink living water

Call to Worship
Pastor: If faith has been a family tradition, it may be we are thirsty for a more personal encounter with Christ.

People: Many of us have grown up in the church. We feel at home here. Perhaps that familiarity hinders what God would like to do with us.

Pastor: God would like to satisfy our thirst by revealing our sins so he can forgive us. Then we can really worship him!

People: We desire to empty our lives of all distractions, that God may fill us with his presence!

Collect
O God of love, who offers an everflowing fountain of forgiveness: Fill our emptiness with your love; that in drinking freely your water of life, we may know the joy of true worship and righteous living. We pray in the name of Jesus, our Savior. Amen.

Prayer of Confession
Worship almost becomes a habit, Father; and we do not feel our spiritual thirst is quenched. It is too easy for us to go through our ritual of worship, and contiue in a lifestyle of sin. Forgive us for worship which is artificial, preventing us from drinking the life-giving water of salvation. Reveal our sins to us, and then cleanse us; that we may be refreshed with your gift of new life in Christ Jesus our Lord, in whose name we pray. Amen.

Hymns
"I Heard the Voice of Jesus Say"
"Jesus Is Tenderly Calling"
"My Hope Is Built"
"'Tis So Sweet to Trust in Jesus"

THIRD SUNDAY IN LENT

First Lesson: Exodus 17:3-7
Theme: Hardened hearts and God's salvation

Call to Worship

Pastor: There is a very ugly side to human nature: God guides, protects, and loves us. Yet we find it so easy to rebel against him.

People: God blesses us so much, that when we must face hardships, we feel he has deserted us.

Pastor: When the Israelites complained to Moses about not having water, God proved he had not deserted them and gave them water from a rock.

People: We know our sinfulness hurts God. Yet in Christ, he forgives our sins and gives us living water.

Collect

Most merciful Father, who led your children of old through the wilderness, and who leads your children today through all kinds of hardships: Melt the hardness of our hearts; that we may not bring you hurt, but give you the joy of our love and devotion. We pray in our Savior's name. Amen.

Prayer of Confession

You have blessed us beyond our ability to be blessed, Father; and so we occupy ourselves with finding fault and voicing our complaints. Forgive us for hardened hearts when we ought to be bubbling over with joy for our redemption. Make the refreshing salvation of Christ known to us, that our thirst for righteousness may be quenched. In his name we pray. Amen.

Hymns

"Come, Thou Fount of Every Blessing"
"God of the Ages, by Whose Hand"
"Guide Me, O Thou Great Jehovah"
"Lead Us, O Father"

THIRD SUNDAY OF LENT

Second Lesson: Romans 5:1-11
Theme: The Spirit-controlled life

Call to Worship

Pastor: When it comes to living by God's laws, we are all condemned sinners.

People: But Christ has erased our guilt by condemning sin for us; and has given us his Spirit to lead us.

Pastor: The choice is still ours: to have either our minds controlled by human nature which results in death, or to have our minds controlled by the Spirit which results in life and peace.

People: We pray for God to help us live by his Spirit that we may be pleasing to him.

Collect

Almighty God, whose Son gives hope to those condemned by your laws: Make us children who desire to have our minds controlled by your Spirit instead of our human nature, that we may receive your gift of life and peace. In our Savior's name we pray. Amen.

Prayer of Confession

We want to be your children, Father; but we seem possessed by our human nature. We know we have not kept your laws, but we also fail to live by your Spirit. Forgive us for our disobedience and sinfulness which deny our allegiance to you. Give us a new life in union with Christ; that we may resist the influence of our human nature, and let your Spirit control us. We pray in Jesus' name. Amen.

Hymns

"Dear Master, in Whose Life I see"
"Holy Spirit, Truth Divine"
"O Come, and Dwell in Me"
"Take My Life and Let It Be"

THIRD SUNDAY IN LENT

Gospel: John 4:5-26 (27-42)
Theme: In the presence of Jesus

Call to Worship

Pastor: Harvest seems far away when we plant our crops. Judgment too, seems far away to make us feel safe in our sins — until we meet Jesus.

People: We do not feel safe in our sins when we find ourselves in the presence of Christ. He convinces us of our guilt.

Pastor: That is for our own good. He reveals our sins so we can accept his forgiveness and be delivered in the day of judgment.

People: We want to meet our Savior and feel his forgiveness cleansing our lives.

Collect

O God, our forgiving Father, who confronts us in our sin with a desire to save us from condemnation: Bring us into the presence of your Son; that we may know from personal experience that he is our Savior. In his name we pray. Amen.

Prayer of Confession

We live from day to day, Father, not too concerned about the consequence of our sinful behavior. Judgment almost seems like a dream from the unreal world; and so we do pretty much as we please. Forgive us for not receiving Christ as one who reveals our sins to us here and now. Forgive us for ignoring his presence and the redemption he brings. Help us to live new lives, reflecting the presence of Christ and his forgiveness. In his name we pray. Amen.

Hymns

"I Am Coming to the Cross"
"I Need Thee Every Hour"
"Nearer, My God, to Thee"
"O For a Closer Walk with God"

FOURTH SUNDAY IN LENT

First Lesson: 1 Samuel 16:1-13
Theme: David is anointed King

Call to Worship

Pastor: When God chooses people to serve him, he looks not at our outward appearance, but in our heart.

People: Hearts that are responsive to God are more important than the physical appearance of greatness.

Pastor: David was responsive to God in his heart. And God chose him to be king of Israel.

People: May our hearts be in tune with our Lord, that he may use us in his service.

Collect

Almighty God, who looks on the heart of those you call to serve you: Make our hearts responsive to your needs, that we may serve you faithfully in the work you would have us do. We pray through Christ our Lord. Amen.

Prayer of Confession

We have not considered ourselves to be your anointed servants, Father; and so we have not been too faithful in our service. Forgive us when we have witnessed to our faith by outward appearance instead of with responsive hearts. Mold us after your will; that our lives may bear fruit in your service. In our Savior's name we pray. Amen.

Hymns

"Forth in Thy Name"
"Lord, Speak to Me"
"O Jesus, I Have Promised"
"Take Up Thy Cross'

FOURTH SUNDAY IN LENT

Second Lesson: Ephesians 5:8-14
Theme: Walk as children of light

Call to Worship

Pastor: As sinners, we wander in darkness. But with Christ leading us, we become children of light.

People: We have spent too much time in darkness. We want to live in the light of Christ.

Pastor: If we live in the light of Christ, we enjoy a life of goodness, righteousness, and truth.

People: May Christ bless us with the light of his love!

Collect

O Father of love: You have blessed us with the light of your Son who calls all who will follow him out of the darkness of sin. Accept us as your children, that we may not try to hide in our sins, but come into the brightness of your redemption. We pray through Christ our Redeemer. Amen.

Prayer of Confesison

We want the light of your love, Father; but we are still attracted to sins which keep us in darkness. Forgive us for wanting to live in both worlds when you have called us out of darkness to be children of light. Teach us your ways, that we may learn the joy of living in the light of Christ our Lord, through whom we pray. Amen.

Hymns

"Come, Every Soul by Sin Oppressed"
"O Master, Let Me Walk with Thee"
"Walk in the Light"
"When We Walk with the Lord"

FOURTH SUNDAY IN LENT

Gospel: John 9:1-41
Theme: Sight for spiritual blindness

Call to Worship

Pastor: Spiritual blindness is the refusal to see that we need God's forgiveness.

People: We are all blind to some degree and need God to open our eyes, that we may see our sin and his love.

Pastor: Christ is the light which shines upon us, giving us the sight we need.

People: May Christ shine his light upon us, and heal our spiritual blindness.

Collect

O Lord God, our heavenly Father, who heals the blindness of man's sinful behavior by the light of your only Son, Jesus our Savior: Touch our hearts, that our spiritual sight may be restored, letting us see clearly the life you are calling us to live. In our Savior's name we pray. Amen.

Prayer of Confession

There are scales on our eyes which need to be removed, Father, so we can see the truth of righteous living. Our spiritual blindness confuses us so that we feel justified living an uncommitted life. Forgive us for our spiritual blindness and then acting as though we could see clearly. We pray for Jesus to give us sight, that we may be healed, and live as those on whom Christ's light has shone. In his name we pray. Amen.

Hymns

"Amazing Grace"
"Ask Ye What Great Thing I Know"
"Open My Eyes, That I May See"
"The Whole World was Lost"

FIFTH SUNDAY IN LENT

First Lesson: Ezekiel 37:1-14
Theme: The valley of dry bones

Call to Worship

Pastor: When hope is overcome by despair, we have the assurance that God restores life.

People: We cling to that assurance because there are times when death would be a better description of our existence.

Pastor: We are not the first to feel that way. Israel one time felt like a valley of dry bones, and God's message was that they would come to life!

People: Our God is full of life! And we know he wants to share it with us. Praise his name!

Collect

O merciful God, who blesses your children with new life: Resurrect us through faith in your Son, that life may become a living experience of joy and happiness. We pray through Christ, our resurrection hope. Amen.

Prayer of Confession

Life is a new gift each day, Father; but sin ruins it, and what we have left is hardly what we can call living. Forgive us for playing into the hands of that which takes away the very thing we need. Breathe into us the life of your Spirit; that we may come alive with hope and happiness. In our Savior's name we pray. Amen.

Hymns

"Have Faith in God, My Heart"
"Hope of the World"
"Jesus, My Strength, My Hope"
"My Hope Is Built"

FIFTH SUNDAY IN LENT

Second Lesson: Romans 8:6-11
Theme: Resurrection to newness of life.

Call to Worship

Pastor: Resurrection is an everyday possibility for us!
People: Every day that we let God's Spirit live in us, he raises us from the death that sin would lead us to.
Pastor: Our bodies will die, but God's Spirit gives us life: a rewarding experience both now and after death.
People: We commit our lives to Christ; that we may live according to his will, not ours.

Collect

Almighty God, whose gift of your Spirit revives those who are dead in sin: Grant us your Spirit; that we may be raised above the influence of our human nature into the likeness and love of your Son our Savior, through whom we pray. Amen.

Prayer of Confession

We are not resurrection conscious, Father, because we think that happens only after death. We have not considered the daily effect that sin has on us; and we are not nearly alive as we could be. Forgive us for dying through sin, and being satisfied without the wonderful life we could be living. Give us a resurrection experience now, that we may be lifted out of the power of sin and into the joy of your presence. We pray in the name of Christ our Lord. Amen.

Hymns

"I Need Thee Every Hour"
"I Want a Principle Within"
"Sing Them Over Again to Me"
"We Are Climbing Jacob's Ladder"

FIFTH SUNDAY IN LENT

Gospel: John 11:(1-16) 17-45
Theme: The raising of Lazarus

Call to Worship

Pastor: Jesus' confidence in life after death as he approached the cross can be ours.

People: The grief felt at Lazarus' death was overcome by the reassurance of Jesus who said, "I am the resurrection and the life."

Pastor: Jesus raised Lazarus from death, showing us that death is not beyond the hope of resurrection.

People: We are strengthened in our faith by Christ's power to raise the dead to life. We believe we shall live with him.

Collect

Eternal God: In the fear and grief we feel at death, you have come with the hope of life through your Son. Prepare us in our hearts for the joy and certainty of being raised into eternity by the power of your Son who is the resurrection and the life. In his name we pray. Amen.

Prayer of Confession

We do not know what it is to die, Father. And so we are filled with fear and avoid facing the reality of our own death. Forgive us for our spiritual immaturity which lets death frighten us. Convince us of our mortality, but also of your gift of immortality; that we may come to Christ in the assurance that he will raise us in glory to be with you. In his name we pray. Amen.

Hymns

"I Know Not How That Bethlehem's Babe"
"I'll Praise My Maker While I've Breath"
"On Jordan's Stormy Banks I Stand"
"The Day of Resurrection"

SIXTH SUNDAY IN LENT
(Passion Sunday)

First Lesson: Isaiah 50:4-9a
Theme: God enables his Servant to endure

Call to Worship

Pastor: Jesus' passion was the result of his hearers not believing the message God had given him.

People: He came as Savior to rule in the hearts of humanity. But he was despised, rejected, and finally crucified.

Pastor: But God did not give man the last word. God proved Jesus' divine message and mission was authentic.

People: We are witness to that! Christ is our Lord and Savior. Praise his name!

Collect

Eternal God, who enabled your Son to be true to his mission, fulfilling his role as our Savior: Give us hearts responsive to his message; that we may receive him as Lord and Savior, and give him the honor and praise which is his. In his name we pray. Amen.

Prayer of Confession

We bless you, O God, for the gift of your Son. But the praise we feel now is not always the attitude of our hearts. Our everyday routines wear down our spiritual enthusiasm, and we are like those who are insensitive to the excitement of Christ as Lord. Forgive us for sporadic faith, and short term discipleship. Capture the spark of faith within us, and kindle it into an eternal flame of love and devotion. We pray through Christ our Lord. Amen.

Hymns

"Beneath the Cross of Jesus"
"O Worship the King"
"Ride On, Ride On in Majesty"
"Savior, Thy Dying Love"

SIXTH SUNDAY IN LENT
(Passion Sunday)

Second Lesson: Philippians 2:5-11
Theme: Jesus, humiliated and glorified

Call to Worship

Pastor: Even though Jesus was the Son of God, he gave up his glory to become a servant.

People: He willingly became one of us, and even humbled himself with death on the cross.

Pastor: Therefore God has glorified him forever in his heavenly kingdom;

People: That at the name of Jesus every knee should bow, and every tongue confess that Jesus Christ is Lord!

Collect

Eternal God, whose Son left his glory with you to be humiliated in our world; but whom you have exalted in your kingdom: Accept our praise and devotion for the sacrificial death of your Son. May the faith we profess reflect an honest allegiance to him as our Savior and King. In his name we pray. Amen.

Prayer of Confession

So often, God, we take for granted the life and death of Jesus, because we know he is your Son. Forgive us when we fail to comprehend the pain and suffering he endured in order to deliver us from the death of sin. Help us to live righteously in thanksgiving for our Lord's willingness to die in our place. In our Savior's name we pray. Amen.

Hymns

"All Praise to Thee, for Thou, O King Divine"
"At the Name of Jesus"
"Crown Him with Many Crowns"
"What Wondrous Love Is This"

SIXTH SUNDAY IN LENT
(Passion Sunday)

Gospel: Matthew 26:14—27:66 or 27:11-54
Theme: The Passion narrative

Call to Worship

Pastor: This is the week of Jesus' passion. Our worship first directs us to his triumphant entry.

People: But the plan to destroy Jesus soon developed, and he was treated as a criminal instead of a king.

Pastor: Jesus' passion mirrors our sinful behavior, but also reveals God's plan of salvation.

People: Jesus Christ is King! May our lives witness to the devotion we profess.

Collect

Gracious Father, whose Son allowed himself to be treated as a criminal that we may be treated as sinless: Reveal the depth of love which Jesus expressed through his passion; that we may open our hearts to his rule over our lives. In his name we pray. Amen.

Prayer of Confession

We find it easy, Father, to praise Jesus as King. But we do not find it easy to admit that our sins betray his authority over us. Forgive us for the passion narrative which our lives record of Jesus. Give us a pilgrimage this week which will re-establish us in the Faith. Then send us as disciples of the victorious Christ, through whom we pray. Amen.

Hymns

"All Glory, Laud, and Honor"
"Hosanna, Loud Hosanna"
"O Sacred Head, Now Wounded"
"There Is a Green Hill Far Away"

SIXTH SUNDAY IN LENT
(Palm Sunday)

First Lesson: Isaiah 50:4-9a
Theme: The suffering Savior

Call to Worship

Pastor: Lift up your hearts in praise to Jesus, King of our lives!

People: We praise Jesus, Son of God, Savior of the world, King of our lives!

Pastor: Jesus ascended his throne by way of the cross. And now he has authority over sin itself.

People: Jesus is King because he has conquered sin, and rules in our hearts. Praise his name!

Collect

Almighty God, whose Son endured the shame of the cross to give us the crown of life: Let the praise of our lips come from the depth of our hearts as we give honor and glory to your Son. Thus may we be honest in the allegiance we profess when we call him King. In his name we pray. Amen.

Prayer of Confession

We have dared to say, Jesus is King, O God. But a king has subjects who are expected to be loyal to him. Our loyalty is more in question than was his kingship when he rode into Jerusalem. Forgive us when we talk one way and live another when it comes to allegiance to Christ. Take full possession of our lives, and lead us in a life of discipleship that will prove once and for all, Jesus is indeed the King of our lives. In his name we pray. Amen.

Hymns

"All Hail the Power of Jesus' Name"
"Lead On, O King Eternal"
"Lift Up Your Heads, Ye Mighty Gates"
"Ride On, Ride On in Majesty"

SIXTH SUNDAY IN LENT
(Palm Sunday)

Second Lesson: Philippians 2:5-11
Theme: Christ humbled and exalted

Call to Worship

Pastor: Glory, blessing, and honor be to Jesus Christ, the Son of God!

People: Christ is our King! We offer ourselves in homage to him.

Pastor: We worship Jesus, because he gave up his likeness to God and came among us to save us.

People: We open our hearts to Christ, that the King of glory may come in. Praise him! Praise him! Praise him!

Collect

Almighty God, Father of our Lord Jesus Christ, who chose to empty himself of glory, that we might be filled with your love: Lift up the King of glory before us; that we may worship and honor him, and publicly proclaim him as Lord of our lives. In his name we pray. Amen.

Prayer of Confession

Christ gave up his glory to be our Savior, Father, because it was sins such as ours which humiliated him on the cross. But you have restored him to the place of highest honor! We believe that; but our lives do not show the honor which Christ deserves. Forgive us for locking up faith in our minds, instead of letting it burst forth in our living. Warm our hearts, and loosen our tongues; that the whole world may know Christ is our Lord, and Lord of all creation! In his name we pray.

Hymns

"All Praise to Thee, for Thou, O King Divine"
"At the Name of Jesus"
"O For a Thousand Tongues to Sing"
"Rejoice, the Lord Is King"

SIXTH SUNDAY IN LENT
(Palm Sunday)

Gospel: Matthew 21:1-11
Theme: Jesus hailed as King

Call to Worship
Pastor: This is the day to let your heart take control of your lips.

People: We can't keep silent. Our hearts are bursting with praise for Jesus, King of our lives.

Pastor: In spite of the shadow of the cross over the palm-strewn way, Jesus rules in the hearts of those who surrender to him.

People: We commit ourselves wholly to Jesus, and ask him to have his way with us.

Collect
O Lord God, whose Son followed your will, both as Servant and as Savior; and now rules in the hearts of those who accept him as King: Open our hearts to his rule; that we may rejoice in the blessings of his kingdom, and share with those who honor him with their lives. In his name we pray. Amen.

Prayer of Confession
We have praised your Son, O God, but not enough. We have loved him, but not enough. We have served him, but not enough. Forgive our weak loyalty. Strengthen our discipleship; that our lives will become effective means of witnessing to others of the wonderful love you have shared with our world through your Son, in whose name we pray. Amen.

Hymns
"All Glory, Laud and Honor"
"Hosanna, Loud Hosanna"
"So Lowly Doth the Savior Ride"
"Take the Name of Jesus with You"

MONDAY IN HOLY WEEK

First Lesson: Isaiah 42:1-9
Theme: First Servant Song: A compassionate Servant

Call to Worship

Pastor: Sinners such as you and I make it necessary for God to send his Servant to redeem us.

People: We are guilty of sin, and suffer the consequence of our sins.

Pastor: God has sent his Servant, Jesus, to have compassion on us, and deliver us from the power of sin.

People: Bless the Lord, O my soul, for his compassionate love in Christ Jesus his Son!

Collect

O God of compassion, who has sent your Son to deliver those who are imprisoned by sin: Release us from our bondage to sin; that we may share in your new covenant of grace and mercy provided by your Son, our Savior, in whose name we pray. Amen.

Prayer of Confession

We have eyes to see, Father, but sin distorts our vision of that which is holy. We crave freedom, but sin makes us captives. We need your compassionate love, O God, to deliver us, and reclaim us as your children. Forgive us for our sins which oppress us as we struggle to come alive. Give us the blessing of your Son who came to minister on our behalf, that we may rejoice in your glory. In his name we pray. Amen.

Hymns

"Depth of Mercy"
"Holy Ghost, Dispel Our Sadness"
"O Love Divine, That Stooped to Share"
"There Is a Balm in Gilead"

MONDAY IN HOLY WEEK

Second Lesson: Hebrews 9:11-15
Theme: Christ, the perfect sacrifice

Call to Worship

Pastor: If God had offered only one covenant, there would be no atonement for our sins.

People: There is no way we can make atonement for our sins against God's laws in his first covenant.

Pastor: The supreme sacrifice for sin has been made for us by Jesus. It is his sacrifice which saves us under the new covenant.

People: We depend on God's grace which he shares so freely in this new covenant through his Son.

Collect

Glorious Father, whose grace is sufficient for our salvation because of your Son's sacrificial death on our behalf: Receive us as children of your new covenant; that we may enjoy the blessings you have promised through Jesus your Son, in whose name we pray. Amen.

Prayer of Confession

We are so helpless, Father, when we try to defend ourselves against sin. There is no sacrifice we can make that will atone for our sins. But we come confessing that we are sinners, and we ask you to forgive us. Forgive us for Christ's sake, who offered himself as the one perfect sacrifice for our sins. Share your grace with us in a covenant relationship which will bind us to you in love, even into eternity. We pray in our Savior's name. Amen.

Hymns

"Alas! and Did My Savior Bleed"
"Amazing Grace"
"There Is a Fountain"
"When I Survey the Wondrous Cross"

MONDAY IN HOLY WEEK

Gospel: John 12:1-11
Theme: The example of sincere devotion to Christ

Call to Worship

Pastor: The mind is important in living the Christian life; but devotion to Christ is often a matter of the heart more than the mind.

People: Sincere devotion to Christ expresses itself in spontaneous love that does not wait for mental instructions.

Pastor: The mask of false piety, or love inhibited by logic and reason, prevent the devotion our Lord deserves.

People: May we be free to give honest devotion which expresses the genuine love we have for Christ.

Collect

Almighty God, who has shown us the depth of your love in the sacrificial ministry of your Son: Inspire our hearts with freedom to demonstrate our love and devotion, that we may be sincere in the faith and worship we express with our lips. In our Savior's name we pray. Amen.

Prayer of Confession

We are people with emotions, Father, but we are afraid our emotions will conflict with our intelligence. So our devotion is controlled by what we think rather than by what we feel. Forgive us for love we have felt, but which we suppressed. Forgive us for love we have expressed, but which we did not feel in our hearts. Strengthen us by your Spirit to be honest and sincere in our devotion to your Son, that faith may not become a passive religious ritual. In his name we pray. Amen.

Hymns

"Jesus, I My Cross Have Taken"
"Jesus, the Very Thought of Thee"
"Lord Jesus, I Love Thee"
"Truehearted, Wholehearted"

TUESDAY IN HOLY WEEK

First Lesson: Isaiah 49:1-7
Theme: Second Servant Song: A Servant to the world

Call to Worship

Pastor: Jesus personifies the Servant of God which Isaiah has prophesied to Israel.

People: He came with the message, and the means of salvation for all who would hear him.

Pastor: His mission is to be a light to the nations revealing God's salvation to the ends of the earth.

People: His light has shone upon us. May we share in his mission, that all in our world may hear and believe.

Collect

Father in heaven, whose love reaches to every person, and who has revealed that love in your Son, Jesus: Keep us in the light of your love; that we may not drift into the darkness of sin, deprived of the blessing of your salvation. We pray through Christ our Lord. Amen.

Prayer of Confession

We bow before you in worship, Father, and the magnitude of our sins is revealed to us. Sin keeps us from seeing the truth of righteous living; but your Son sheds light upon us, and we see ourselves as we really are. Forgive us for our sinful attitudes and behavior. Lead us in the paths of righteousness, that we, too, may be a light to the world, revealing your salvation to all mankind. In our Savior's name we pray. Amen.

Hymns

"Break Forth, O Living Light of God"
"Brightly Beams Our Father's Mercy"
"Christ for the World We Sing"
"O Spirit of the Living God"

TUESDAY IN HOLY WEEK

Second Lesson: 1 Corinthians 1:18-31
Theme: The cross is God's power to save sinners

Call to Worship

Pastor: The cross, once a disgrace, has become the symbol of God's power to save sinners.

People: The cross has meant death for many, because of humanity's judgment. But for many more, it means salvation, because of God's love.

Pastor: The cross of Christ is where human sin meets with God's love; and God's love, contrary to reason, defeats sin.

People: Our faith is founded, not on reason, but on God's love and power to save us by our Lord's death on the cross.

Collect

O loving Father: You have taken humanity's act of cruelty and turned it into your act of grace. Guide us in our spiritual pilgrimage to the cross of Christ; that we may not stumble over reason and logic, failing to receive the salvation which awaits us at the foot of the cross. We pray through Christ, our crucified Lord. Amen.

Prayer of Confession

We do not identify ourselves with those who think the cross is foolishness, Father. But neither do we surrender ourselves to the full power of your salvation. We tolerate sin, and justify ourselves with pious attitudes. Forgive us for our indifference to the price our Lord has paid to cleanse us from all unrighteousness. Strengthen us in committed living; that our lives may witness to our personal salvation accomplished by Christ's death on our behalf. In his name we pray. Amen.

Hymns

"Beneath the Cross of Jesus"
"Cross of Jesus, Cross of Sorrow"

TUESDAY IN HOLY WEEK

Gospel: John 12:20-36
Theme: Christ lifted up

Call to Worship

Pastor: There is no Christ without a cross. That is why Jesus came.

People: God turned the shame of the cross into the glory of redemption when Jesus was lifted up.

Pastor When Jesus was lifted up on the cross, that was only a preview of the glory to come when he would be lifted up into heaven.

People: That is a glory we all look forward to as we follow Jesus in his suffering.

Collect

Eternal God, whose Son was lifted up in shame that we might be lifted up with him in glory: Keep us steadfast in our walk with Jesus; that we may follow his path from death into life, where we shall forever enjoy the glory of his presence. In our Savior's name we pray. Amen.

Prayer of Confession

O God, we tend to follow Jesus until the cross comes into view. Then we falter in our discipleship, although we never forget the glory on the other side of the cross. Forgive us when we depart from our Savior on his path of sorrow he too' in order to give us a home in glory. Keep us close to Ch ; that through life and death, we may finally experience the 'ory of living in your kingdom. In Jesus'name we pray. Am 1.

Hymns

"Am I a Soldier of the Cross"
"Are Ye Able"
"Jesus, Keep Me Near the Cross"
"O For a Faith that Will Not Shrink"

WEDNESDAY IN HOLY WEEK

First Lesson: Isaiah 50:4-9a
Theme: Third Servant Song: The obedient Servant

Call to Worship

Pastor: Our Lord faced a difficult ministry when he came to proclaim salvation.

People: We praise his name for his faithfulness to God, when humanity was so cruel to him.

Pastor: Jesus was obedient to the mission God gave him, because he trusted God to fulfill his promise of salvation.

People: That promised salvation is ours, because Christ was obedient even to death. Thanks be to God for our Lord Jesus Christ!

Collect

Almighty God, whose Son obediently fulfilled his mission to bring salvation, even when rejected by those he came to save: Make us aware of the resistance we unconsciously express; that we may arise to a new sense of commitment, and respond wholeheartedly to your salvation. In our Savior's name we pray. Amen.

Prayer of Confession

We are dependent on our Lord's obedience to the mission you gave him, Father. He was faithful to death, yet we are so careless with the new life to which he saved us. Forgive us for our unconcern about our sinful attitudes which deny his Lordship over our lives. Increase our responsiveness to our Lord's mission, that his obedience may result in our salvation. In his name we pray. Amen.

Hymns

"Alas! and Did My Savior Bleed"
"O Love Divine, What Hast Thou Done"
"O Sacred Head, Now Wounded"
"What Grace, O Lord, and Beauty Shone"

WEDNESDAY IN HOLY WEEK

Second Lesson: Hebrew 12:1-3
Theme: Encouraged in discipleship

Call to Worship

Pastor: Life imposes many crosses for us to bear; but our faith gives us the fortitude to press on.

People: Our faith is in Jesus who defeated the power of his cross, and turned it into victory for all who put their faith in him.

Pastor: Our Lord's victory has revealed the glory of God's love for those who are steadfast in their discipleship.

People: We are encouraged by our Lord's example, and strengthened by his Spirit. May our discipleship demonstrate loyalty and depth of faith.

Collect

Almighty God, whose Son faced his cross without wavering, and defeated its power and shame: Grant us renewed faith in our discipleship by his example; that we, too, may endure our crosses with victory, and experience the glory of your love. In our Savior's name we pray. Amen.

Prayer of Confession

We become discouraged so easily, Lord, when our faith is challenged by unbelief, or direct criticism. We want to avoid conflict and so limit our discipleship to the protected areas of life. Forgive us when we have sacrificed our faith on the crosses of opposition and ridicule. Renew our faith, and strengthen our discipleship; that we may be true in all circumstances to our Savior, Jesus Christ, in whose name we pray. Amen.

Hymns

"Jesus, Keep Me Near the Cross'
"Take Up Thy Cross"
Chorus: "Turn Your Eyes Upon Jesus"
"What Wondrous Love Is This?"

WEDNESDAY IN HOLY WEEK

Gospel: John 13:21-30
Theme: Judas plans for the betrayal

Call to Worship

Pastor: As Jesus prepared to eat the Passover meal with his disciples, he knew Judas was planning to betray him.

People: Judas had made his decision, and Jesus had to face the consequence of the evil plot.

Pastor: Jesus knew God would use that evil to share his love with our world.

People: God's love is redemptive in spite of man's evil plans. We claim that redemption, and pray for faithfulness to Christ.

Collect

Heavenly Father, whose Son was betrayed by one of his closest followers: Keep us secure in your love, and firm in our faith, that we may not submit to any form of false allegiance or insincere discipleship. We pray in Jesus' name. Amen.

Prayer of Confession

Dear Father, we pause to consider the hurt that Jesus felt when he was betrayed and crucified. And in our meditation, we feel the finger of accusation pointing at ourselves. Forgive us when we lose hold of faith, making ourselves vulnerable to the persuasive power of selfish gain. Establish us in the faith, strongly committed to Christ as Lord, that we may be true in our discipleship. In our Savior's name we pray. Amen.

Hymns

"Go to Dark Gethsemane"
"In the Hour of Trial"
"More Love to Thee, O Christ"
"O Jesus, I Have Promised"

THURSDAY IN HOLY WEEK
[Maundy Thursday]

First Lesson: Exodus 12:1-14
Theme: Institution of the Passover

Call to Worship

Pastor: We share in this sacred feast to celebrate our Lord's redeeming love.

People: We rejoice in our deliverance from sin granted by the blood of the Lamb.

Pastor: We celebrate as Christians, because our Lord delivers us from sin, just as God delivered the Israelites from Egypt.

People: God's deliverance finally brought them to the promised land. God is delivering us, too, to the promised life of redemption in Christ. Praise his name!

Collect

O God, our great Deliverer: You have found us in bondage to sin, and have sent your Son to deliver us. Receive us as your children, by faith in the blood of Christ, shed on our behalf; that we may enter your promised salvation. In our Savior's name we pray. Amen.

Prayer of Confession

We tremble in your presence, O God; for we know our life is a daily record of sin. But we claim the blood of Christ as our hope of redemption, not by any righteousness of ours, but by your grace promised through him. Hear our confessions, Father, for we have let sin control our lives. Forgive us for our unrighteousness, and deliver us to a new life in which Christ has control. For his sake we pray. Amen.

Hymns

"Here, O My Lord, I See Thee"
"Jesus, Thy Blood and Righteousness"
"O Love Divine, What Hast Thou Done"

THURSDAY IN HOLY WEEK
[Maundy Thursday]

Second Lesson: 1 Corinthians 11:23-26
Theme: The Lord's Supper

Call to Worship

Pastor: The holy sacrament of our Lord's Supper is prepared for our participation.

People: We come to our Lord's table, not because of our righteousness; but because of our thankfulness for being saved from sin.

Pastor: We eat and drink in memory of Jesus, proclaiming his death as the seal of God's new covenant.

People: By grace, God receives us and forgives us. By faith, we claim that forgiveness, and rejoice in God's new covenant.

Collect

Gracious Father, who has brought us into a new covenant by the blood of your Son, our Savior: Grant us the blessing of your Spirit as we commune at your table, that our participation will be a faithful witness to the love you offer to all who will receive Jesus as Lord and Savior. In his name we pray. Amen.

Prayer of Confession

Father, we are your children, but our sins have warped that relationship. We come as sinners, confident of your love to reclaim us as your children. Forgive us for all that denies your Fatherhood. Let the witness of our faith now proclaim our real identity as we eat and drink in memory of our Savior's sacrificial and atoning love. In his name we pray. Amen.

Hymns

"Alas! and Did My Savior Bleed"
"Beneath the Forms of Outward Rite"
"Come, Every Soul by Sin Oppressed"

THURSDAY IN HOLY WEEK
[Maundy Thursday]

Gospel: John 13:1-15
Theme: the example of humility

Call to Worship

Pastor: Draw near with faith as we gather around our Lord's table to celebrate our Savior's love.

People: We come in memory of our Savior's love; knowing he humbled himself on our behalf.

Pastor: When Jesus washed his disciples' feet, he set for us the example of humility which he expects us to follow.

People: May our communion with Christ confirm us in a life of humble service to others.

Collect

Most merciful Father, who desires that we humble ourselves in willing service to our fellow man: Help us to follow Christ's example of assuming the servant role, that we may not let ourselves become proud or self-righteous in our faith. We pray through Christ who humbled himself on our behalf. Amen.

Prayer of Confession

We see these sacred elements, Father, and are reminded that we still have much to learn of our Lord's lesson in humility. Forgive us for our pride which causes us to accept the name of Christ without following the way of Christ. Share your grace with us; that we may learn the virtue of humility, and experience the peace of a humble heart. In our Savior's name we pray. Amen.

Hymns

"Here, O My Lord, I See Thee"
"In Memory of Our Savior's Love"
"O the Depth of Love Divine"
"What Wondrous Love Is This"

GOOD FRIDAY

First Lesson: Isaiah 52:13—53:12
Theme: Fourth Servant Song: The redemptive Servant

Call to Worship

Pastor: The Son of God has died in our place. He lived without sin; but in his death, he bore the sins of all humanity.

People: He was despised and rejected, the outcast of society. Yet his sacrifice atones for our sins.

Pastor: Jesus' death gives us redemption because God sent him to save us from sin. And Jesus was faithful to that mission.

People: Our hearts are heavy because of our Lord's suffering. But we rejoice at the same time, because our Lord's death brings God's gift of new life.

Collect

Father in heaven, who grieves over the sins of humanity, yet whose love provides forgiveness in the atoning death of your Son: Convict us of our sins against your love, and convince us of your desire to forgive, that our Lord's death may fulfill your purpose in our lives. In the name of Christ we pray. Amen.

Prayer of Confession

What pain and sorrow we must bring to you, Father. And yet what love you pour out to us! Forgive us for what we have let sin do to us, contrary to your created purpose. Cause us to see that our modern ways of avoiding your Son are no better than nailing him to the cross. Transform our hearts, our minds, our whole nature, to live in full commitment to Christ our Redeemer, in whose name we pray. Amen.

Hymns

"Alone Thou Goest Forth"
"Jesus, Keep Me Near the Cross"

GOOD FRIDAY

Second Lesson: Hebrews 4:14-16; 5:7-9
Theme: Jesus, our great high priest

Call to Worship

Pastor: We celebrate our Lord's death, not as one taken from us, but as one who takes us to God.

People: Jesus is like a high priest who enters the very presence of God, and intercedes on our behalf.

Pastor: Through his death, Jesus atones for our sins, inspiring us to return to God, assured of his grace.

People: We come to the throne of God, knowing we will find mercy and grace sufficient for our sins.

Collect

Gracious Father, who has given your Son to intercede on our behalf: Inspire us with devotion and steadfastness, that we may accept the atonement which Jesus provides through his death. In his name we pray. Amen.

Prayer of Confession

We are bold to come before you, Father, even though we are guilty of sin. We come because your Son, our Savior, has opened the way into your presence. So hear us as we confess our sinfulness, and forgive us for the sake of Christ who pleads on our behalf. Cleanse us of our unrighteousness; and strengthen us for committed discipleship. In our Savior's name we pray. Amen.

Hymns

"Cross of Jesus, Cross of Sorrow"
"Majestic Sweetness Sits Enthroned"
"O Sacred Head, Now Wounded"
"Savior, Thy Dying Love"

GOOD FRIDAY

Gospel: John 18:1-19:42 or 19:17-30
Theme: Arrest, trial, and death of Jesus

Call to Worship

Pastor: Jesus died because of religious people like you and me.

People: Religion too easily becomes an act we perform, rather than a way of life to which we commit ourselves.

Pastor: Jesus' death destroys any reason to pretend with faith; and it challenges us to take up our cross and follow our Master.

People: Our faith is in Christ who forgives us, strengthens us, and call us into discipleship.

Collect

Almighty God, who suffers through the agony of seeing your Son rejected by those he is trying to save: Grant that our faith may be a sincere acceptance of your Son; that we may cease to bring you hurt, and avail ourselves of the forgiveness of our crucified Lord, in whose name we pray. Amen.

Prayer of Confession

Today we are especially conscious of how sinful we are, Father, and how forgiving you are toward us. We are moved to repentance and confession, truly grieved by our sinful behavior. Forgive us for acting religious, when in our hearts we resist the faith we try to portray. Inspire us to surrender our wills to Christ, that his death may bring us into eternal life. In his name we pray. Amen.

Hymns

"Behold, the Savior of Mankind"
"Beneath the Cross of Jesus"
"On a Hill Far Away"
"There Is a Green Hill Far Away"

EASTER DAY

First Lesson: Acts 10:34-43
Theme: Christ's resurrection is for all people

Call to Worship

Pastor:　For nearly two thousand years, Christians of each generation have thrilled with the celebration of Easter.

People:　What God has done in Christ benefits all persons who believe in him.

Pastor:　God raised Jesus from the dead. And we are privileged to proclaim his gospel to our generation.

People:　Jesus is Lord! May the whole world know of his power to forgive sins, and be raised to new life!

Collect

Eternal God: Your Son, Jesus, conquered the grave, offering forgiveness to all persons. Pour out your Spirit upon us as we worship our risen Lord; that we may join that vast throng of followers who rejoice in his power, which not only conquers the grave, but defeats the curse of sin. We pray through Christ our Lord. Amen.

Prayer of Confession

With thanksgiving in our hearts, we come into your sanctuary, O God; because we know that Christ's resurrection is the source of our hope. Without him we are dead in our sins. Because of him, we are raised to new life with you. Forgive our carnal nature which works against resurrection faith. Restore us in love; revive our faith; renew our commitment, that our discipleship may be a living witness to Christ's resurrection. In his name we pray. Amen.

Hymns

"Come, Ye Faithful, Raise the Strain"
"Sing with All the Sons of Glory"
"The Day of Resurrection"

EASTER DAY

Second Lesson: Colossians 3:1-4
Theme: Resurrection Living

Call to Worship

Pastor: Christ is risen from the dead, and lives among us, bringing hope and joy to all who believe in him.

People: We rejoice because we have been raised to new life with Christ!

Pastor: Such life is full of joy because we put to death the earthly desires which contradict God's will, and become new persons in Christ.

People: Christ is our life! We commit ourselves to resurrection living as we put off our sinful desires and put on our new nature.

Collect

Most gracious Father, whose power over sin and death raises us to a new life in Christ: Fill our minds with Christlike desires; that we may put to death our earthly desires, and live a new life in fellowship with our risen Lord, through whom we pray. Amen.

Prayer of Confession

We are full of praise, Father, for Christ's resurrection. But our praise is due more to a fear of death, than to love for life. We want security as we prepare for death, but we have put to death the joy of being alive. Forgive us for dying in sin, when you would make us alive in Christ. Raise us out of sin's power into the wonderful love of Christ; that fear of death may have no opportunity to lay hold of us. We pray through Christ, our risen Lord. Amen.

Hymns

"Christ Jesus Lay in Death's Strong Bands"
"Christ the Lord Is Risen Today"
"I Know that My Redeemer Lives"
"Now the Green Blade Riseth"

EASTER DAY

Gospel: John 20:1-18 or Matthew 28:1-10
Theme: Christ's resurrection

Call to Worship

Pastor: Death could not conquer the tremendous power of life in our Lord and Savior!

People: For three days Jesus let death have its way, only to prove he had power over the grave.

Pastor: Our Lord's resurrection is the sign that we, too, shall pass through death into life if we follow him as Lord, and trust him as Savior.

People: Our faith is in Jesus Christ who rose from the dead, who lives in our hearts, and who will bring us into his eternal presence! Praise his name!

Collect

Victorious Father, who surrendered your Son to death, only to raise him from the grave; that we may know the hope of eternal life which is available to all who believe: Give us faith which will inspire committed living; that in death we may be forever with our Savior, in whose name we pray. Amen.

Prayer of Confession

Father, our Lord's tomb was empty because death could not hold him in its grip. He arose to show us the victory which can be ours. But sin's power to destroy us threatens that victory. Forgive us for professing resurrection faith, but denying it with sin-motivated living. Raise us above the sin dominated life, to a life firmly established in the faith of our living Lord, through whom we pray. Amen.

Hymns

"Good Christian Men, Rejoice and Sing"
"Jesus Christ Is Risen Today"
"Low in the Grave He Lay"
"O Sons and Daughters, Let Us Sing"

SECOND SUNDAY OF EASTER

First Lesson: Acts 2:14a, 22-32
Theme: The early church proclaims Christ's resurrection

Call to Worship

Pastor: The first generation Christians did not hesitate to preach the good news of Christ's resurrection.

People: They knew what they had seen; and they knew God had sent them to tell others what he had done in Christ.

Pastor: God is still doing a mighty work through his church. We, too, must witness to God's redemption for our world.

People: God give us strength and wisdom to share our resurrection faith with our world!

Collect

Eternal God, who raised your Son in glory, and who inspired your church to preach the good news: Use us as your messengers to proclaim the gospel truth; that people, dying in sin, may yet be restored to glorious living. In our Savior's name we pray. Amen.

Prayer of Confession

We believe Jesus' resurrecton ought to be told to the ends of the earth, Father. But our tongues are tied when we are asked to share our faith. Forgive us for the silence of our lips when others depend on us to interpret the Christian faith. Loosen our tongues, and use our lives to inspire others to look to Christ for salvation, that our friends may not be lost to sin by our negligence. In Christ's name we pray. Amen.

Hymns

"Go Make of All Disciples"
"I Love to Tell the Story"
"O For a Thousand Tongues to Sing"
"Sing with All the Sons of Glory"

SECOND SUNDAY OF EASTER

Second Lesson: 1 Peter 1:3-9
Theme: Joy in Salvation

Call to Worship

Pastor: Thanks be to God our Father, who blesses us with new life by raising Jesus from the dead!

People: With joy, we look forward to the rich blessings God has promised out of his great mercy.

Pastor: Let us confirm our faith in Christ then, whatever may be our trials, assured that salvation is ours.

People: Whatever may test our faith, we are convinced of God's love, and will be true to him.

Collect

Heavenly Father, who fills us with joy over our new life you have given by raising Jesus from the dead: Keep us strong in the faith; that we may not become disheartened by trials or testing, forgetting our salvation is in Christ, our risen Lord, through whom we pray. Amen.

Prayer of Confession

Christ has been raised to life, Father, and through his resurrection you raise us to new life. That fills us with joy, Father, until our faith is tested. Then we lose hope, and our salvation does not make us rejoice. Forgive us when our faith is so superficial that it is easily threatened by difficulties in life. Strengthen our faith in your grace, that our risen Lord may keep us sure of the salvation he provides. In his name we pray. Amen.

Hymns

"Good Christian Men, Rejoice and Sing"
"O Happy Day, That Fixed My Choice"
"Rejoice, the Lord Is King"
"Rejoice, Ye Pure in Heart"

SECOND SUNDAY OF EASTER

Gospel: John 20:19-31
Theme: Faith is believing without seeing

Call to Worship

Pastor: The Christian faith is founded on the resurrection of our Lord, an historic and spiritual reality.

People: We believe he arose from the dead, and raises us to new life which continues beyond the grave.

Pastor: We who have not seen Jesus, believe because the early church believed what they saw and proclaimed in each generation.

People: We believe what we have heard, because God through his Spirit has given us the faith to believe. Thanks be to God!

Collect

Almighty God: You raised Jesus from the dead and inspired the early church to proclaim your truth! Establish us in the faith; that our witness may help others to believe without seeing, and live by faith in our risen Lord, through whom we pray. Amen.

Prayer of Confession

We are happy, Father, because we have believed without seeing. And faith has been real! But we cannot say we never have doubts. We have our moments when we need a special word to assure us. Forgive us when we question the source of our faith, and its validity. Continue to be in our midst, encouraging us, convincing us, and inspiring us; that our lives may be a growing and maturing experience in faith. We pray through Christ our Lord. Amen.

Hymns

"O Holy Savior, Friend Unseen"
"Pass Me Not, O Gentle Savior"
"Strong Son of God, Immortal Love"
"Thine Is the Glory"

THIRD SUNDAY OF EASTER

First Lesson: Acts 2:14a, 36-41
Theme: Peter preaches repentance and baptism

Call to Worship

Pastor: If we were to be honest in our confessions, our sins would accuse us of being enemies of Christ.

People: Sin has possessed us, but we long to be set free in order to love and serve our Lord.

Pastor: The church continues to proclaim God's eternal truth: Repent and be baptized in the name of Jesus.

People: We believe in Jesus; and are convinced he will forgive us, and enable us by the Holy Spirit to be Christian disciples.

Collect

Almighty God, who gives your Holy Spirit to those who repent and are baptized: Make faith a genuine response in our hearts; that, by true repentance, and a sincere acceptance of baptism, we may receive the gift of your Holy Spirit. In our Savior's name we pray. Amen.

Prayer of Confession

Many facts prevent us from believing the truth about ourselves, Father. We live in a Christian nation; we have a Christian background; and we support the church. But the truth is, we are sinners. In religious ritual, we repent; but it fails to speak for the sins we hide in our hearts. Wash us clean with your forgiveness, that our confirmation of Christian baptism may be an honest invitation for your Holy Spirit to be in control of our lives. Hear us for Jesus' sake. Amen.

Hymns

"Dear Lord and Father of Mankind"
"Just as I Am, Without One Plea"
"How Can a Sinner Know"
"Take My Life, and Let It Be Consecrated"

THIRD SUNDAY OF EASTER

Second Lesson: 1 Peter 1:17-23
Theme: Be holy because of what Christ has done

Call to Worship

Pastor: We pray to God, believing he is our Father and divine Judge. Therefore we should show reverence to him by the way we live.

People: We know God is our Father, because he has revealed himself to us in Jesus, our Savior.

Pastor: Jesus, who was sinless, has redeemed us from sin by his sacrificial death on our behalf.

People: God raised Jesus in glory, defeating the power of sin, and inspires us to live holy lives in obedience to the Christian hope.

Collect

Gracious Father, who has redeemed us by the perfect sacrifice of your Son: Make firm our faith in the glorious resurrection of Jesus; that we may live holy and reverent lives in thanksgiving for our salvation. We pray through Christ, our risen Savior. Amen.

Prayer of Confession

Forgive us, O God, for our affirmations of faith which call you Father, contradicted by our demonstrations of life which deny we are your children. Bring our faith and works into harmony, that our lives may show true reverence for you as our God. Assure us of your forgiveness, and guide us into true holiness. We pray in Jesus' name. Amen.

Hymns

"I Want a Principle Within"
"Jesus, Thine All-Victorious Love"
"Lord, I Want to Be a Christian"
"Take Time to Be Holy"

THIRD SUNDAY OF EASTER

Gospel: Luke 24:13-35
Theme: The Emmaus Road

Call to Worship

Pastor: What a happy morning! The risen Lord is with us, wanting to reveal himself to us.

People: We desire that more than anything; because too often we go through life wishing he were nearer.

Pastor: Christ is always by our side trying to make his presence felt, but too often we are on "the road to Emmaus," and do not see him.

People: May our eyes be opened to the presence of our risen Lord!

Collect

Almighty God: In the vastness of your creation, you know the paths we walk daily. And on these paths your risen Son comes to walk with us! Give us clear vision, open hearts, and understanding minds, that we may know our risen Lord is with us. In his name we pray. Amen.

Prayer of Confession

Dear Father, how often our risen Lord has been in our midst, and we did not know it. We have walked by his side, and so often did not invite him into our lives. Weak faith has permitted our eyes to be closed, and we did not know we were blind. Forgive us for these sins against the resurrection. Open our eyes, that faith may convince us Christ is risen indeed! In his name we pray. Amen.

Hymns

"Open My Eyes, That I May See"
"Talk with Us, Lord"
"Walk in the Light"
"When We Walk with the Lord"

FOURTH SUNDAY OF EASTER

First Lesson: Acts 2:42-47
Theme: Fellowship of believers

Call to Worship

Pastor: Christ's church is a fellowship of believers who care for one another as brothers and sisters.

People: God has made us a family of brothers and sisters to share in each others joys and sorrows.

Pastor: The church is a family where each must feel loved, and each must share their love with others.

People: May Christ's church always be a fellowship wherein we manifest the caring love for one another that Christ has shared with us.

Collect

Gracious God, who by your Spirit has called your church to be a fellowship of believers, bound together in mutual care and concern: Inspire us individually to be caring persons; that together we may be your church in ministry to one another with sincere love and service. In our Savior's name we pray. Amen.

Prayer of Confession

We give thanks to you, O God, for your church. Within its fellowship we are nurtured in faith. But also within its fellowship we manifest our human nature, and wound the spirits of our brothers and sisters in Christ. Forgive us when we deny our divine nature, and ignore your call to care for one another. Help us to be a church within these walls, and around the world, which will be a true refuge where love and concern is obvious and genuine. In Jesus' name we pray. Amen.

Hymns

"All Praise to Our Redeeming Lord"
"Blest Be the Tie that Binds"
"In Christ There Is No East or West"
"Jesus, United by Thy Grace"

FOURTH SUNDAY OF EASTER

Second Lesson: 1 Peter 2:19-25
Theme: Be patient in suffering

Call to Worship

Pastor: Life includes many experiences which bring us undeserved suffering.

People: We find it difficult to accept such trials. But we believe God will give us endurance.

Pastor: Jesus was without sin; and yet he suffered on our behalf that we might have wholeness. His example enables us to endure suffering.

People: Suffering has its way of bringing God's blessings to us. May God keep us faithful at such a time.

Collect

Almighty God: Your Son was without sin; and yet he suffered death on our behalf, that we might receive life. Encourage us by his example; that we too, may be faithful when hurt by unjust suffering. We pray through Christ our Lord. Amen.

Prayer of Confession

We are so sensitive to pain, Father, especially when we do not understand the reasons why. We find it undesirable to suffer as Christians must sometimes suffer; and therefore we have not received blessings that could have been ours if we had followed the example of Christ. Forgive us for our unwillingness to accept, as Christ did, our suffering. Give us endurance; that we may trust completely in your redemptive love and protection. In the name of Christ we pray. Amen.

Hymns

"Am I a Soldier of the Cross"
"In the Hour of Trial"
"Must Jesus Bear the Cross Alone"
"O For a Faith that Will Not Shrink"

FOURTH SUNDAY OF EASTER

Gospel: John 10:1-10
Theme: Jesus leads his followers into abundant life

Call to Worship

Pastor: We trust Jesus because he is faithful in meeting our spiritual needs as Lord and Savior.

People: As a shepherd is faithful to the needs of his sheep, so Jesus is faithful to us.

Pastor: Life is filled with happiness, because Jesus saves us from all that destroys the joy of living.

People: We have tried the false gods of happiness, and have suffered their deception. But in Christ, we experience the joy he gives to those who follow him!

Collect

O God of joy and happiness, who desires to save your children from needless hurts and empty living: Enable us to hear your Son calling us into his fold; that we may enjoy the wonderful life of being in his presence. In his name we pray. Amen.

Prayer of Confession

We desire Christ to be our Shepherd, Father; but we have wanted freedom to choose our own paths. And that freedom has robbed us of the joy of being alive. Forgive us, Father, and draw us back into our Lord's love and protection. Renew us with life that is full of joy, assured by the presence of our Savior, the great Shepherd of his sheep, through whom we pray. Amen.

Hymns

"All the Way, My Savior Leads Me"
"He Leadeth Me: O Blessed Thought"
"Savior, Like a Shepherd Lead Us"
"Shepherd of Eager Youth"

FIFTH SUNDAY OF EASTER

First Lesson: Acts 7:55-60
Theme: The stoning of Stephen

Call to Worship

Pastor: The message of Christ was proclaimed by the early church, even when persecution cost their lives.

People: We remember the commitment of Stephen, the first Christian martyr, who gave his life for the cause of Christ.

Pastor: We remember Stephen, also because he prayed for his persecutors, among whom was Saul, who later became a great missionary.

People: We praise God for the faith of the early Christians which produced a growing fellowship of believers in spite of persecution.

Collect

Eternal God, our Father: Your church has survived the storms of persecution, flourishing on the very forces that would destroy it. Deepen our commitment to your church, that our faith and conduct may turn the indifference of our generation into a growing fellowship of believers. In Jesus' name we pray. Amen.

Prayer of Confession

Dear Father, we rejoice in the fact that your church is alive in our world today. We know that it could not be if it were not for the sacrifices of apostles who knew your church would outlast the forces that opposed them. Forgive us when we have not seen the real forces we are striving with today. Give us the courage of those engaged in serious battle, that we may give your church renewed growth in our society. We pray through Christ. Amen.

Hymns

"A Mighty Fortress Is Our God"
"Faith Of Our Fathers"

FIFTH SUNDAY OF EASTER

Second Lesson: 1 Peter 2:2-10
Theme: Rid yourselves of evil and be God's people

Call to Worship
Pastor: Consider the sins that remain a part of your life-style, and get rid of them!

People: We have experienced the Lord's kindness, and need to grow in Christian living.

Pastor: Let God use you to establish his kingdom on earth, that others who do not know God's mercy may receive it.

People: We are God's people whom he has called out of sin to proclaim his good news to our world. May our lives give glory to Christ our Savior.

Collect
O God our Father: You have called us from death to life; from darkness to light; from sin to righteousness! Give us power to come alive in our witness to your wonderful deeds; that we may become your temple where Christ is honored as Lord and Savior. In his name we pray. Amen.

Prayer of Confession
By grace, you have saved us from sin, Father. But by poor commitment, we return to the sins which keep us from growing in Christ. Forgive us for abusing your mercy, and continuing in our old ways. Lead us out of our darkness into your marvelous light, where we can become living stones in the church of our Lord and Savior, Jesus Christ, through whom we pray. Amen.

Hymns
"Christ Is Made the Sure Foundation"
"Lord, I Want to Be a Christian"
"Love Divine, All Loves Excelling"
"O Jesus, I Have Promised"

FIFTH SUNDAY OF EASTER

Gospel: John 14:1-14
Theme: Jesus prepares the disciples for his departure

Call to Worship

Pastor: It was a sad experience for the disciples when Jesus spoke of leaving them.

People: They could not understand why Jesus had to leave, or how they could find their way to God.

Pastor: They soon learned that Jesus had to leave so he could return and minister through his church, bringing many into God's presence.

People: The risen Lord continues to do wonderful works for those who believe. It is through him that we find God.

Collect

Heavenly Father, whose Son is the only way by which we can find you: Reveal yourself to us through Jesus; that we may have the assurance of your presence enabling us to do the work our Lord has directed us to do. In our Savior's name we pray. Amen.

Prayer of Confession

Our Father, we too, have spent much time with Jesus, but have the same feeling that we know too little about you. Forgive us for separating the ministry of Jesus from your self-revelation in him. Open our minds and hearts to the faith you are trying to establish in us; that we may be effective in our ministry on your behalf. We pray through Christ our Lord. Amen.

Hymns

"Blessed Assurance, Jesus Is Mine"
"O Son of God Incarnate"
"Spirit of Faith, Come Down"
"Thou Art the Way: To Thee Alone"

SIXTH SUNDAY OF EASTER

First Lesson: Acts 17:22-31
Theme: The message of salvation is preached to the Gentiles

Call to Worship

Pastor: The good news of Christ is that all people have been called to salvation.

People: God has promised and is faithful to his promises. Jesus came to set all people free from sin.

Pastor: All who believe in him whom God raised from the dead are set free from sin's power.

People: We are free by the grace of God! May our risen Lord enable us to live in the grace of God!

Collect

Almighty Father, who chose the Hebrew race to be your messenger of salvation to the Gentile world: Use your church as the new Israel, that we may be your light to our world, revealing your salvation through Christ Jesus, our Lord, in whose name we pray. Amen.

Prayer of Confession

Our Father, we know Christ's redemption is for the whole world. We are involved in world mission, but we confess our personal feelings sometimes interfere with that worldwide approach. Forgive us when we support far away missions, in absentia, but close the door of salvation to nearby neighbors who do not meet our doctrinal standards. Help us to see the human worth, and savability of all persons; not because of guidelines we establish, but because of your love expressed in Jesus, our Savior, through whom we pray. Amen.

Hymns

"Brightly Beams Our Father's Mercy"
"O Thou Who Art the Shepherd"
"Rescue the Perishing"

SIXTH SUNDAY OF EASTER

Second Lesson: 1 Peter 3:13-22
Theme: Be faithful with your Christian witness

Call to Worship

Pastor: It is God's grace that saves us from sin and enables us to live the Christian life.

People: We are often tempted to react contrary to God's grace when unbelievers challenge us.

Pastor: We represent Christ, and out of reverence for him we need to confront our adversaries with love and kindness.

People: May God give us the grace to be Christlike, so those who ridicule the Christian faith will be put to shame.

Collect

Gracious Father, who calls us to live a life which exemplifies your grace as we witness to others: Fill us with kindness toward those who are critical of our faith; that with a clear conscience, we may demonstrate the grace by which you have redeemed us from our unrighteousness. We pray through Christ our Lord. Amen.

Prayer of Confession

We enjoy the fellowship of Christian friends, Father, because we feel strengthened in our faith. But when we are offended by those who do not share our faith, we are not only hurt, but often we become angry. Forgive us for our unkind attitudes toward those who ridicule us, or make us uncomfortable. Keep us true to the faith, and faithful in our witness, but always in the spirit of gentleness, with the grace which you have expressed so freely in our Lord and Savior, Jesus Christ, in whose name we pray. Amen.

Hymns

"A Charge to Keep I Have"
"Forth in Thy Name"
"Savior, Teach Me Day by Day"

SIXTH SUNDAY OF EASTER

Gospel: John 14:15-21
Theme: Jesus promises the Counselor

Call to Worship

Pastor: God has given his Spirit to be with us forever, just as Jesus promised.

People: The Spirit of truth is our Counselor, helping us when we are lonely, discouraged, or afraid.

Pastor: God expresses his love by sharing his Spirit with us. He also asks us to express our love through obedience to Jesus.

People: God forbid that we should ever fail to follow the life of love our Lord commands. May the Holy Spirit enable us to give such obedience.

Collect

Eternal God, who is ever by our side, encouraging us with your Holy Spirit: Enable us to give obedient love to our Lord; that we may grow in faith, strengthened by the help of your Spirit. In Jesus' name we pray. Amen.

Prayer of Confession

Dear Father, we do love your Son, Jesus. But we confess our love does not always produce obedience. And disobedience prevents us from enjoying the blessings of your Holy Spirit. Forgive us for our weak love and disobedient living. Pour out your Spirit upon us, that we may be enabled to give honest love to Jesus, and receive the promised support of your Spirit. We pray through Christ our Lord. Amen.

Hymns

"Come, Ye Disconsolate"
"Holy Spirit, Truth Divine"
"Joys Are Flowing like a River"
"When We Walk with the Lord"

ASCENSION DAY
(Or the Sunday Nearest)

First Lesson: Acts 1:1-11
Theme: The ascension of Jesus

Call to Worship

Pastor: Jesus, whom God raised from the dead, was taken into heaven as his disciples watched.

People: The ascension of Jesus was the crowning event in his ministry.

Pastor: It was also the beginning of a new ministry for the church. The whole world became a mission field in which the church is sent to be witnesses of the risen Lord.

People: God help us accept our mission, that we may prepare our world for our Lord's final triumph when he returns.

Collect

Father in heaven, who glorified your Son through his ascension, and who continues to glorify him through the witnessing faith of his church: Make us sensitive to our mission, that we may convince others to accept him as Lord and Savior. In his name we pray. Amen.

Prayer of Confession

We are thankful for being a part of the world-wide church, Father. And we are thankful for those who witness to the risen Lord, enabling faith to reach to the ends of the earth. But we know there are still persons whose salvation depends on our witness. Forgive us for words unsaid, and love not shared. Revive us with zeal to be living witnesses of our risen Lord, that we may lead many into your kingdom. In our Savior's name we pray. Amen.

Hymns

"All Hail the Power of Jesus' Name"
"Come, Let Us Rise with Christ"
"Crown Him with Many Crowns"

ASCENSION DAY
(Or the Sunday Nearest)

Second Lesson: Ephesians 1:15-23
Theme: Christ is exalted above all other powers

Call to Worship

Pastor: Christ our Lord now sits at the right hand of God the Father, with glory and honor!

People: Glory be to God who has made his Son supreme Lord over all things.

Pastor: God's great power with which he glorified his Son is the same power at work in us, enabling us to be his church at work in our world as the body of Christ.

People: May God give his Spirit to us, that we may know the wonderful blessings of being his church.

Collect

Almighty God, who has exalted your Son with the highest honor and glory: Inspire your church with wisdom and power, that the exalted Christ may be honored as Lord of all. In his name we pray. Amen.

Prayer of Confession

Father, we are your church, the body of Christ, serving our world. And your power which was manifested in the risen Christ, whom you lifted into heaven, is the very power undergirding your church today. Forgive us for turning our backs to you, and then trying to stir up enough strength on our own to keep the church going. Lift our hearts and minds to things above where Christ is; that he may display his position of authority in the church, and in the world. In his name we pray. Amen.

Hymns

"Hail, Thou Once Despised Jesus"
"Look, Ye Saints! The Sight Is Glorious"
"Majestic Sweetness Sits Enthroned"
"The Head That Once Was Crowned"

ASCENSION DAY
(Or the Sunday Nearest)

Gospel: Luke 24:46-53
Theme: The great commission

Call to Worship
Pastor: Our Lord's last message before he was lifted into heaven was his charge to go to all people inviting them into discipleship.

People: The church in every age has accepted that commission to baptize and teach in the name of Christ.

Pastor: Our Lord has not left us alone to carry out that assignment. He is with us at all times to help us in our ministry.

People: Inspired by our Lord's presence, we desire to share the gospel with our world.

Collect
Gracious Father, whose Son has commissioned his followers to go into all the world with the gospel: Guide and uphold the church with his presence, that we may reach the unreached with our Lord's message of redemption. In his name we pray. Amen.

Prayer of Confession
We believe in a world-wide church with a world-wide mission, Father. But we neglect the commission Christ gave to us. We send missionaries to represent us; but our tight purse strings represent our resistance to our Lord's commission. Forgive us for hiding behind benevolent offerings which do not express true benevolence. Burden our hearts with the importance of being in mission at home and overseas, that we may do the work our Lord has sent us to do. In his name we pray. Amen.

Hymns
"Christ for the World We Sing"
"Go, Make of All Disciples"
"O Zion, Haste"

SEVENTH SUNDAY OF EASTER

First Lesson: Acts 1:6-14
Theme: Prayer

Call to Worship

Pastor: After Jesus' ascension, the Apostles often gathered to pray together in expectation of the Holy Spirit.

People: Prayer is God's way of opening our hearts to his love and power.

Pastor: We are strengthened when we pray together, because it unites us with God our Father, and binds us together as brothers and sisters in Christ.

People: May God move us to be a praying congregation, open to the inspiration of the Holy Spirit.

Collect

Heavenly Father, who imparts your wisdom, power, love, and grace to those who commune with you in prayer: Join our hearts together in a praying fellowship; that we may receive the blessing of your Spirit, and find strength to be your church at work. We pray through Christ our Lord. Amen.

Prayer of Confession

We would never question the power of prayer, Father. But we are willing to get along with too little of the strength you provide in prayer. Forgive us for our breakdown in spiritual communion, which results in our ineffective discipleship. Revive our faith in prayer; and make us aware of its necessity in the fellowship of Christians; that through prayer, we may become strong in the faith. We pray through Christ our Lord. Amen.

Hymns

"Sweet Hour of Prayer"
"Take Time to Be Holy"
"Talk with Us, Lord"
"What a Friend We Have in Jesus"

SEVENTH SUNDAY OF EASTER

Second Lesson: 1 Peter 4:12-14; 5:6-11
Theme: Rejoice when suffering for Christ

Call to Worship

Pastor: Commitment to Christ has often caused persons to suffer rejection and abuse.

People: Suffering is not always in the form of persecution; but it tempts us to deny our faith nevertheless.

Pastor: If we suffer because of our faith, we should rejoice that God has given us such faith, and trust him to give us endurance.

People: We trust God to keep us faithful when being a Christian brings rejection.

Collect

Our Father in heaven, whose children are often in conflict with those who do not believe, and therefore suffer because of their faith: Make firm our faith; that our witness will be sure, and any suffering due to our witness will not weaken our faith. We pray through Christ our Lord. Amen.

Prayer of Confession

We are not being persecuted as was the early church, Father; so we feel safe in our faith. But we resist the unkindness of society; and we protect ourselves from being hurt by those who do not share our faith. And in our defense, we deny our faith. Forgive us for weakening, instead of growing, when we feel our faith brings rejection or pain. Fill our hearts with joy for being a part of the Christian fellowship of believers; and use us even when ridiculed, to bear witness to your love. In our Savior's name we pray. Amen.

Hymns

"Am I a Soldier of the Cross"
"Be Not Dismayed"
"He Who Would Valiant Be"

SEVENTH SUNDA ⁄F EASTER

Gospel: John 17:1-11
Theme: Jesus prays for his disciples

Call to Worship

Pastor: As Jesus approached his hour, he prayed for his disciples to be faithful.

People: They believed in Jesus, but needed God's help to carry out their work of convincing others about Jesus.

Pastor: The church is in the world, but not of the world, to show that Christ is the source of life.

People: May the witness of our congregation give glory to our Lord Jesus Christ.

Collect

Gracious Father, whose Son was glorified not only in his sacrificial death, but also through the faithfulness of his followers: Keep us safe from all temptation; that we, too, may be true to our calling, and give glory to your Son our Savior, in whose name we pray. Amen.

Prayer of Confession

We serve in a nation which is familiar with the Christian faith, Father. And the cries of persons who need the ministry of the church are not heard over the noise of the church making itself at home in the world. Forgive us for our likeness to the world, when we have been called to transform the world by our likeness to Christ. Make us receptive to the power of your Spirit, that we may be the source of help in our world for which Christ prayed. In his name we pray. Amen.

Hymns

"God of Grace and God of Glory"
"Love Divine, All Loves Excelling"
"One Holy Church of God Appears"
"Walk in the Light"

THE DAY OF PENTECOST

First Lesson: Isaiah 44:1-8
Theme: God alone is God

Call to Worship

Pastor: All praise to the only God, our Creator, Redeemer, and Judge!

People: Only God can create. Only God can redeem. Only God can judge our sins.

Pastor: There is none other to whom we will pray; in whom we will put our trust; and with whom we shall live forever!

People: Glory be to God our Father, who has shared his Son to be our Savior and his Spirit to be our Companion!

Collect

Eternal God, who alone possesses the power of our Creator, the love of our Redeemer, and the wisdom of our final Judge: Defend us against all temptation to yield to the influence of any feeling that would hinder our devotion to you; that we may sincerely give true worship and service in your honor. We pray through Christ our Lord. Amen.

Prayer of Confession

Heavenly Father, we are the handiwork of your creative and redeeming love. Forgive us when our obedience and loyalty deny that our ultimate destiny is in your hands. Help us to honor you with true praise and devotion, that your majesty may be recognized throughout the world. In the name of Christ we pray. Amen.

Hymns

"All People that on Earth Do Dwell"
"Holy, Holy, Holy! Lord God Almighty"
"O God, Our Help in Ages Past"
"O Worship the King"

THE DAY OF PENTECOST

Second Lesson: Acts 2:1-21
Theme: Descent of the Holy Spirit at Pentecost

Call to Worship

Pastor: The Spirit of the Lord is upon us; for he has made us his church, and has called us to be his witnesses.

People: We are sent to bear witness to the love of God revealed through Jesus his Son, whom he raised from the dead.

Pastor: God enables us to be faithful to our calling by giving us his Spirit to be our source of power.

People: May God find us receptive to his Spirit, that he may equip us to fulfill our mission as his church.

Collect

O God, our heavenly Father, who gives life and power to your church through the gift of your Spirit: Inspire us with your Spirit to bear witness to our living Lord; that those to whom you send us may understand the good news of Christ, and accept their salvation. In our Savior's name we pray. Amen.

Prayer of Confession

It is easy for us to find fault with the church, our Father, because we are distracted by its human characteristics. Forgive us for denying ourselves the power of your Spirit which could do mighty things through the church in spite of our faults and weaknesses. Send your Spirit upon us with power and enthusiasm; that we may be a living church, proclaiming a living faith in a living Lord. We pray through Christ our Lord. Amen.

Hymns

"Blest Be the Tie That Binds"
"Jesus, United by Thy Grace"
"O Spirit of the Living God"

THE DAY OF PENTECOST

Gospel: John 20:19-23
Theme: Empowered with the Holy Spirit

Call to Worship

Pastor: Our Lord has called his church to be in ministry, sharing his peace with our world.

People: Our hearts are full of joy because we have experienced the peace our Lord gives.

Pastor: Jesus empowers us with the Holy Spirit, and sends us forth in his name, that others may also enjoy his peace.

People: May the Holy Spirit be our strength, enabling us to share the peace our Lord gives.

Collect

O holy Father, whose Son has commissioned his church to be in his service, giving us the Holy Spirit to be our support: Send us into our community with power to witness on behalf of Christ; that those who hear may respond in honest confession of sin, and receive your forgiveness. In our Savior's name we pray. Amen.

Prayer of Confession

You have blessed us with the peace of Christ, O God, and our hearts are glad. But in our gladness, we have not heard clearly enough the call to share our joy with others. And so we reject the gift of your Spirit which would enable us to go forth in Christ's name. Fogive us for depriving ourselves of the joy of serving others; and depriving others of knowing the peace of Christ. Breathe upon us the breath of new life, that we may be strengthened by your Spirit in all our endeavors. In Christ's name we pray. Amen.

Hymns

"Breath on Me, Breath of God"
"See How Great a Flame Aspires"
"Spirit of Faith, Come Down"
"Spirit of God, Descend upon My Heart"

FIRST SUNDAY AFTER PENTECOST
(Trinity Sunday)

First Lesson: Deuteronomy 4:32-40
Theme: Remember what God has done

Call to Worship

Pastor: God reveals himself to us, that we may know he is with us.

People: God redeems us from sin, that we may know he loves us.

Pastor: God calls us to respond with faith and obedience, that he may know we trust him.

People: We remember many wonderful experiences God has given us. We give ourselves in sincere devotion to his will.

Collect

Father in heaven, who created us in your image, and who redeems that image in us through your Son: Inspire us with your Holy Spirit to respond in obedience to your will that we may experience the fullness of life to which you would save us. In Jesus' name we pray. Amen.

Prayer of Confession

We have experienced your revelation and redemption, O God; but our response lacks the obedience which you desire. Forgive us when we forget your love and ignore your presence with a life of indifference and independence. Give us a clear understanding of the ways in which you give yourself to us for our benefit, that we may give ourselves to you in faithful service. In the name of Christ we pray. Amen.

Hymns

"Ancient of Days"
"Come, Thou Almighty King"
"How Great Thou Art"
"Thanks to God Whose Word Was Spoken"

FIRST SUNDAY AFTER PENTECOST
(Trinity Sunday)

Second Lesson: 2 Corinthians 13:5-14
Theme: Trinitarian blessing

Call to Worship

Pastor: God has so wonderfully expressed himself through the grace of his Son, Jesus.

People: It is through the grace of Jesus that we experience the love which God our Father gives so freely.

Pastor: And this experience of God's love unites us with one another in the fellowship of the Holy Spirit!

People: The grace of our Lord Jesus Christ, the love of God, and the fellowship of the Holy Spirit bring us joys beyond measure!

Collect

Almighty God, who shares your loving kindness through the Father, Son, and Holy Spirit: Draw us into your presence; that we may experience the blessings of your divine nature, and live within the boundaries of your providence. In our Savior's name we pray. Amen.

Prayer of Confession

We enjoy our participation in the Christian faith, Father; for then we are most healthy in body, mind, and soul. But it is too easy for us to withdraw; and then we become weak. Forgive us when we have avoided your presence in our lives, resisting your grace and love, and the fellowship of the Holy Spirit. Restore us to wholeness in the security of your divine presence; that we may know the joy of being your children. In Jesus' name we pray. Amen.

Hymns

"Father, in Whom We Live"
"Holy God, We Praise Thy Name"
"Holy, Holy, Holy"
"We Believe in One True God"

FIRST SUNDAY AFTER PENTECOST
(Trinity Sunday)

Gospel: Matthew 28:16-20
Theme: The great commission

Call to Worship
Pastor: We are people who have been assigned to a great task by our Lord Jesus Christ.
People: We are his church, and he has commissioned us to go to all people to make them disciples.
Pastor: Our goal is to convince them of God's love, baptize them into the Christian faith, and teach them to live the Christian life.
People: We strive toward that goal, because we know our Lord is with us all the time!

Collect
Great God, our Father, whose Son has commissioned us to go into our world to make disciples of all people: Guide and uphold us by your Spirit; that, strengthened for our task, we may be enabled to bear fruit in your kingdom. We pray through Christ our Lord. Amen.

Prayer of Confession
You have called us to be your children, Father; and we respond with faith. But when your Son commissions us to share our faith with others, we find reasons to wait. Forgive us for our resistance to be in mission, hindering the outreach of your church and the new life which could come to others. Remove our hesitancy, and inspire us for discipleship; that our Lord's presence may not be to observe our idleness, but to encourage our ministry. In our Savior's name we pray. Amen.

Hymns
"Go, Make of All Disciples"
"Heralds of Christ"
"O Zion, Haste"
"We've a Story to Tell to the Nations"

PROPER 4
Sunday between May 29 and June 4 inclusive
(If after Trinity Sunday)

First Lesson: Genesis 12:1-9
Theme: Faith to follow God

Call to Worship

Pastor: God has called us to leave behind a life without purpose, and become his people.

People: Our faith assures us God will bless us with his love and kindness.

Pastor: God calls, not only to bless us, but that he may bless others through us.

People: May we follow in faith, and rejoice in the life God is calling us to live.

Collect

Sovereign Lord, who calls us to be your people: Grant us the faith to respond to your bidding; that life may become a fountain of joy for us, as well as as mission to bring joy to others. In our Savior's name we pray. Amen.

Prayer of Confession

You have called us to be your people, O God, but we fear the responsibility required of us. Forgive us when we are not willing to venture in faith with you. Lead us in a life of blessing that will help us reveal your love to our world. In the name of Christ we pray. Amen.

Hymns

"Be Thou My Vision"
"Guide Me, Oh Thou Great Jehovah"
"He Leadeth Me: O Blessed Thought"
"Lead Kindly Light"
Chorus: "Where He Leads Me I Will Follow"

PROPER 4
Sunday between May 29 and June 4 inclusive
(If after Trinity Sunday)

Second Lesson: Romans 3:21-28
Theme: Justified by faith in Christ

Call to Worship

Pastor: We have all sinned against God, and have separated ourselves from his salvation.

People: God's laws make it clear that our sins can bring us only his judgment.

Pastor: But now God has a new way of bringing us into his love, apart from the law. By grace, God saves us through Faith in his Son, Jesus.

People: Our faith is in Jesus, who died for our sins, and brings us into a right relationship with God.

Collect

Gracious Father, whose righteousness has been demonstrated in the death of Jesus as atonement for our sins: Increase our faith in our Savior's love, that we may find your grace sufficient to cover our sins. In our Savior's name we pray. Amen.

Prayer of Confession

We come to you as sinners, Father, confessing that we have let our sins separate us from your glory. Your laws do not make right our sins, but rather make it all the clearer that we are sinners. And so we claim your grace which you have expressed through your Son, Jesus, who died for our sins. Grant us your forgiveness as we confirm our faith in Jesus our Savior, that we may be restored in fellowship with you. We pray in Jesus' name. Amen.

Hymns

"Blessed Assurance"
"I've Found a Friend"
"Jesus, Lover of My Soul"
"Jesus, Thy Blood and Righteousness"

PROPER 4
Sunday between May 29 and June 4 inclusive
(If after Trinity Sunday)

Gospel: Matthew 7:21-29
Theme: The wise and foolish house builders

Call to Worship

Pastor: We have two basic choices in life: either obey God or disobey him.

People: We have learned many ways to appear committed to God, when we are not.

Pastor: We cannot pretend forever. Our obedience finally proves its fidelity, and disobedience receives its just reward.

People: May God help us make our discipleship more than lip service, so that our lives will bear witness to our loyalty.

Collect

Heavenly Father, whose Son, Jesus, spoke not only for us to hear your Word, but to obey it: Convict us of our insincere expressions of faith, and stir us to obedient loyalty, that we may be sure of Christ as our strong foundation. In his name we pray. Amen.

Prayer of Confession

We have been heard to say we are Christians, Father; and we will not deny it. But those who hear our witness, must wonder at times when they see the way we live. Forgive us for our sins of disobedience which do not suport our words of allegiance. Transform our hearts by your Spirit; that both our words and our behavior will witness to our loyalty to Christ, through whom we pray. Amen.

Hymns

"I Would Be True"
"O Jesus, I Have Promised"
"Truehearted, Wholehearted"
"When We Walk with the Lord"

PROPER 5
Sunday between June 5 and 11 inclusive
(If after Trinity Sunday)

First Lesson: Genesis 22:1-18
Theme: Faith and commitment

Call to Worship
Pastor: Life is a test of faith day after day.
People: Day after day God proves himself worthy of our trust.
Pastor: Each day God asks that we put him first in our lives, and give him our full surrender.
People: We trust God to be all that he promises. May we be all that he asks of us.

Collect
O Lord, our great Provider, you have promised to be our God, and have called us to be your children. Give us the faith to let you be our God, and the commitment to live as your children; that we may experience the blessing of a close relationship with you. We pray through Christ our Lord. Amen.

Prayer of Confession
We feel your prodding, Lord, for us to let go and let you be our God. But life has such a grip on us that we find it difficult to come in full surrender to you. Forgive our shallow commitment when we give you only lip service. Give us the strength, courage, and will to live by faith, and to offer true commitment of ourselves to you. In Jesus' name we pray. Amen.

Hymns
"Draw Thou My Soul, O Christ"
"Father, I Stretch My Hands to Thee"
"My Faith Looks Up to Thee"
"O For a Faith That Will Not Shrink"

PROPER 5
Sunday between June 5 and 11 inclusive
(If after Trinity Sunday)

Second Lesson: Romans 4:13-18
Theme: The faith of Abraham

Call to Worship

Pastor: Abraham was a godly person because he had complete faith in God's promises.

People: God accepted Abraham as being righteous because he had that kind of faith in God.

Pastor: We, too, can be accepted as righteous, by putting our faith in Jesus, who died for our sins, granting us redemption.

People: What a wonderful salvation God promises through Jesus! He is our Savior in whom we put our faith.

Collect

Father in heaven, who considers righteous those who believe the promises you make: Give us faith like that of Abraham; that we may be accepted as righteous by our faith in Jesus, who promises forgiveness to all who believe. In his name we pray. Amen.

Prayer of Confession

We want to be considered righteous, Father, but our sins are so many. And when we realize how sinful we are, it is difficult to feel we are justified. Forgive us for our many sins, but especially for our weak faith in the promises of Jesus to redeem us. Lead us into an acceptance of salvation, believing we are forgiven, and therefore accepted as righteous by the grace of Jesus, through whom we pray. Amen.

Hymns

"Have Faith in God, My Heart"
"My Hope Is Built"
"Standing on the Promises"
"'Tis So Sweet to Trust in Jesus"

Sunday between June 5 and 11 inclusive
(If after Trinity Sunday)

Gospel: Matthew 9:9-13
Theme: Jesus demonstrates God's mercy

Call to Worship

Pastor: God accepts us in his service, not by any righteousness of ours, but simply because of his mercy.

People: Our unworthiness prevents us many times from giving ourselves in service to our Lord.

Pastor: Jesus will help us overcome that if we remember he called Matthew, and even sat at table with other religious outcasts.

People: We claim God's mercy, and ask him to use us in his service, forgiving our past sins.

Collect

Gracious Father, whose Son demonstrated your mercy by associating with sinners, even calling them into your service: Convince us of your mercy for us, that we may surrender ourselves to you to be used according to your will. In our Savior's name we pray. Amen.

Prayer of Confession

We believe in your forgiveness, Father; but sin still hinders our total commitment to your service. Forgive us for asking for your forgiveness and then letting our sins have enough power to limit our discipleship. Give us your mercy; that we may respond whole-heartedly, assured of your cleansing, and willing to be in your service. We pray through Christ our Lord. Amen.

Hymns

"Amazing Grace!"
"Come, Thou Fount of Every Blessing"
"Depth of Mercy"
"There's a Wideness in God's Mercy"

PROPER 6
Sunday between June 12 and 18 inclusive
(If after Trinity Sunday)

First Lesson: Genesis 25:19-34
Theme: Accepting our relationship to God

Call to Worship
Pastor: God has made it clear who we are, and whose we
are.
People: We are children of God, and we belong to him.
Pastor: Yes, we are God's children by his choice. And he
wants it to be our choice, too.
**People: May the way we live reveal our praise and thanks-
giving for being a part of God's family!**

Collect
Most merciful God: Like a father who provides for his family, and like a mother who nourishes her babies, you have
chosen us to be your children! Keep us mindful of our identity; that we may live up to our name, and give you honor
and glory, through Jesus Christ our Lord. Amen.

Prayer of Confession
We are grateful, O God, to be your children. But we know
there are many times that we act as though we couldn't care
less. Forgive us when we take so lightly our identity, and give
up our rights and blessings for the sake of other interests.
Help us to live unashamed of who we are, dedicated to main-
taining our family ties. In Jesus' name we pray. Amen.

Hymns
"Children of the Heavenly Father"
"Come, Ye That Love the Lord"
"Lord, I Want to Be a Christian"
"O Jesus, I Have Promised"
"What A Friend We Have In Jesus"

PROPER 6
Sunday between June 12 and 18 inclusive
(If after Trinity Sunday)

Second Lesson: Romans 5:6-11
Theme: Christ died for the ungodly

Call to Worship
Pastor: Because sin controls us, God offers his love to us even as we sin.
People: There would be no hope for us if we have to become righteous before God would accept us.
Pastor: God has taken the initiative to save us through the death of his Son on our behalf.
People: We praise God for his love he gives to us in our sin, through Jesus who died to save us.

Collect
Heavenly Father, whose Son comes to us even as we sin, offering reconciliation with you: Open our hearts to his redemption; that we may be forever in a right relationship with you. We pray in the name of Jesus, who died for us. Amen.

Prayer of Confession
We are your children, Father; but our sins make us your enemies. Our only hope is our Savior, Jesus Christ, who has died in our place. Forgive us for our sinfulness which separates us from fellowship with you. Reclaim us as your children, saved by the grace of our Lord Jesus, through whom we pray. Amen.

Hymns
"Arise, My Soul, Arise"
"Depth of Mercy"
"Jesus, Thy Blood and Righteousness"
"What Wondrous Love Is This"

PROPER 6
Sunday between June 12 and 18 inclusive
(If after Trinity Sunday)

Gospel: Matthew 9:35—10:8
Theme: Jesus' compassion for the helpless

Call to Worship
Pastor: As Jesus preached to his own people, he saw so many who felt as if no one cared about them.

People: Our Lord had compassion on them, and wanted to share God's love with them.

Pastor: In order to share God's love, he needed help. And so Jesus sent his disciples to preach encouragement from God.

People: Our Lord's ministry is just as vital today. We pray that many will assist us in answering God's call to be in mission.

Collect
O loving God, whose Son had compassion on the multitudes who were like sheep without a shepherd: Challenge us with a compassionate ministry for the oppressed and helpless; that many may find hope and salvation in Jesus our Lord, through whom we pray. Amen.

Prayer of Confession
We are so used to seeing people who are depressed and discouraged, Father. And we think of all the social agencies which can help them. But we do not let your love move us to compassion for them. Forgive us for the excuses we make, as we let people wander aimlessly without hope or help. Sensitize your church to the fields of labor beyond our sanctuaries; that we may share the good news of Christ our Shepherd, in whose name we pray. Amen.

Hymns
"Lord of the Harvest, Hear"
"O Thou Who Are the Shepherd"
"We Bear the Strain of Earthly Care"
"With Thine Own Pity, Savior"

PROPER 7
Sunday between June 19 and 25 inclusive
(If after Trinity Sunday)

First Lesson: Genesis 28:10-17
Theme: God renews his covenant with Jacob

Call to Worship

Pastor: God expressed confidence in Jacob even though Jacob was unworthy through sin.

People: As Jacob was running from his sin, God came to him with the assurance of divine protection.

Pastor: God renewed the covenant he had made with Abraham, promising Jacob he would be blessed with God's faithfulness.

People: Like Jacob, may we realize God's presence in our lives, and commit our ways to him.

Collect

O loving God, who obliges yourself in a covenant relationship with your children without any proof of our worthiness: Reveal your covenant love to us, that we may turn from our sins and live a new life in faithfulness to your covenant. Hear us, for Jesus' sake. Amen.

Prayer of Confession

You are our Father, O God, and we are your children who depend on your goodness. But we take your presence for granted, unaware that we live constantly in the midst of your blessings. Forgive us when we sin against your covenant love. Come into our sinful lives, and show us your love, that we may become new persons in Christ Jesus our Lord, through whom we pray. Amen.

Hymns

"Come, Thou Fount of Every Blessing"
"I Sought the Lord"
"Nearer, My God to Thee"
"We Are Climbing Jacob's Ladder"

PROPER 7
Sunday between June 19 and 25 inclusive
(If after Trinity Sunday)

Second Lesson: Romans 5:12-19
Theme: Jesus' grace and Adam's sin

Call to Worship
Pastor: We are all like Adam, in that we are naturally inclined to sin.

People: And our sin, like Adam's sin, leads to death.

Pastor: But God gives us hope through his Son, Jesus, whose death gives life to all who believe in him.

People: The grace of our Lord Jesus Christ is greater than the sin we share with Adam. Praise his name!

Collect
Eternal God, who conquers the power of sin in each generation by your grace poured out in the death of Jesus our Lord: Make firm our devotion to Christ; that our likeness to Adam may be transformed into the image of Christ, in whose name we pray. Amen.

Prayer of Confession
It is so easy for us to be like Adam, Father; and we excuse ourselves by thinking it is natural. But our real desire is to be more like Jesus. Forgive us for our persistence in sin, and our indifference to Jesus' death for our redemption. Grant us understanding and acceptance of the grace of our Lord who gives us the hope of eternal life. In his name we pray. Amen.

Hymns
"How Happy Every Child of Grace"
"Jesus Is All the World to Me"
"Just as I am, Without One Plea"
"O Happy Day"

Sunday between June 19 and 25 inculsive
(If after Trinity Sunday)

Gospel: Matthew 10:24-33
Theme: Be faithful, even if persecuted

Call to Worship

Pastor: Social acceptance is a powerful force which often hinders our Christian witness.

People: We want to share our faith; but we often hesitate, because we are afraid we will be ridiculed.

Pastor: Jesus said we should be more afraid of what God will say about us if we are not true to him.

People: We need more strength to be faithful in our witness. May God help us.

Collect

O Holy God, whose Son challenges us with discipleship which is not threatened by those who reject us or our witness: Increase our faith in your protection; that we may be faithful with our witness, even when fear would make us hesitate. We pray through Christ our Lord. Amen.

Prayer of Confession

We have no desire to deny our faith, O God; but our witness, silenced by fear of rejection, is not adding to your kingdom. Forgive us for such little respect we give to you when we are so easily convinced our witness should be withheld because of possible ridicule. Give us the determination to be true with our witness; that we may be faithful in our commitment to Christ, through whom we pray. Amen.

Hymns

"Are Ye Able"
"In the Hour of Trial"
"O For a Faith that Will Not Shrink"
"Stand Up, Stand Up for Jesus"

PROPER 8
Sunday between June 26 and July 2 inclusive

First Lesson: Genesis 32:22-32
Theme: Struggling with past sin

Call to Worship

Pastor: Often our past gets in our way, hindering God's redeeming love and forgiveness.

People: Our past bothers us, because much of it is contrary to God's will.

Pastor: Struggling with our past is difficult, but God gives us victory through our Lord Jesus Christ!

People: Praise God for a salvation that erases the sins of our past, and gives us a new life for the future with Christ Jesus our Savior!

Collect

God of mercy and grace, you know the inner conflict with past sin so often harasses us. Give us victory in Christ; that once and for all we may turn our backs on the sins of our past, and move forward in faith, assured of a new beginning with Jesus our Savior, in whose name we pray. Amen.

Prayer of Confession

We often have high hopes, Lord, but then our past creeps up, and our high ideals for tomorrow are crushed by the memory of sins in the past. We constantly struggle with who we have been and who we want to become. Forgive us for the power we grant to our past, instead of trusting in the power of your redeeming love. Turn us around to enjoy a new life yet to be created by you, redeemed from a past you have forgiven. In our Savior's name we pray. Amen.

Hymns

"Ask Ye What Great Thing I Know"
"Jesus, Lover of My Soul"
"O Thou, in Whose Presence"
"Thou Hidden Source of Calm Repose"

PROPER 8
Sunday between June 26 and July 2 inclusive

Second Lesson: Romans 6:3-11
Theme: Dead to sin, alive in Christ

Call to Worship

Pastor: When we are baptized into the Christian faith we are baptized into new life in Christ.

People: Christ died on the cross; and our old nature is put to death with him.

Pastor: And because we have died with Christ, we shall also live with him!

People: May God help us be true to our new life in Christ!

Collect

Almighty God, who raised your Son from death to life, giving us power over sin and the grave: Remind us of the faith to which our baptism witnesses, that we may keep ourselves firmly rooted in the new life to which Christ has saved us. In our Savior's name we pray. Amen.

Prayer of Confession

Father, we have died to sin with Christ on his cross. That is our faith. But sin continues to try to get a hold on us; and we have difficulty letting Christ raise us to new life. Forgive us for a witness which denies our baptism, and fails to destroy the power of sin in our lives. Give us faith which is strong enough to convince us of the death and resurrection which Christ has effected within our hearts; that we may truly be alive in Christ Jesus our Lord, through whom we pray. Amen.

Hymns

"I Want a Principle Within"
"Lord, I Want to Be a Christian"
"Love Divine, All Loves Excelling"
"O Come, and Dwell in Me"

PROPER 8
Sunday betwen June 26 and July 2 inclusive

Gospel: Matthew 10:34-42
Theme: The cost of discipleship

Call to Worship
Pastor: Christian discipleship demands complete surrender to Jesus Christ.

People: We confess that, too often, our piety is more in our minds than in our muscle.

Pastor: Jesus is first and last in the lives of his disciples. All that we do or think is based on our commitment to him.

People: May God guide us into total commitment as we consider the cost of discipleship.

Collect
Almighty God, whose Son has given us a very serious call to follow him with complete loyalty: Strengthen our faith in him as Lord and Savior; that we may be willing to bear the cross assigned to us as his disciples. In Jesus' name we pray. Amen.

Prayer of Confession
We want to be disciples of Jesus, Father; but we are frightened when we hear how demanding discipleship really is. So much of our lives seems to be in conflict withwhat you require. Forgive us when we have made decisions based on personal interest, rather than on our commitment to Christ. Help us to establish all our activities as opportunities to be in discipleship for Christ, through whom we pray. Amen.

Hymns
"A Charge to Keep"
"He Who Would Valiant Be"
"My Jesus, As Thou Wilt"
"Take Up Thy Cross"

PROPER 9
Sunday between July 3 and 9 inclusive

First Lesson: Exodus 1:6-14, 22 — 2:10
Theme: Divine providence

Call to Worship
Pastor: Praise be to God for his presence in our past, present, and future!

People: We look where we have been, and we see God's hand; we see where we are, and we know God is here.

Pastor: Tomorrow is yet to be revealed, but it too, is designed by God to fulfill his plan for us.

People: Praise be to God for his presence in our past, present, and future.

Collect
God of all ages, as your story unfolds, life becomes an exciting drama of your divine providence. Grant us steadfastness in our faith to trust in your care; that we may rest assured our destiny is in your hands. In the name of Christ we pray. Amen.

Prayer of Confession
We are fearful creatures, Lord, afraid we may drown in the tempest of life. Forgive us when we focus only on our fears, and become deaf to the hope our faith would instill in us. Help us to see clearly your hand of mercy in the past; to feel your touch of love in our lives today; and to hear your voice inviting us into the future. In our Savior's name we pray. Amen.

Hymns
"All the Way My Savior Leads Me"
"God of Our Life"
"Rock of Ages"
"Tis So Sweet to Trust in Jesus"

PROPER 9
Sunday between July 3 and 9 inclusive

Second Lesson: Romans 7:14-25a
Theme: The conflict of body and soul

Call to Worship

Pastor: We share with St. Paul, the inner conflict between the Spirit and our human nature.

People: We want to do the right, but our human nature makes us sinners.

Pastor: Our help is in Jesus Christ who shared our human nature in order to destroy sin.

People: We want to be united with Christ, that our lives may be controlled by his Spirit.

Collect

O God, our heavenly Father, whose Son took upon himself our nature, that he might condemn sin in the flesh: Enable us to have our minds controlled by your Spirit, rather than by our human nature, that we may experience the life and peace our Savior gives. In his name we pray. Amen.

Prayer of Confession

You know our frustration, Father: We want to be righteous, but we are possessed by sin. Forgive us when our human nature makes it so difficult for us to express the righteousness we desire. Cause us to depend more on Christ to enable us to live the life of the Spirit; that we may not continue with our minds controlled by our human nature. We pray in Jesus' name. Amen.

Hymns

"Be Thou My Vision"
"Dear Master, in Whose Life I See"
"I Need Thee Every Hour"
"Lead Us, O Father"

PROPER 9
Sunday between July 3 and 9 inclusive

Gospel: Matthew 11:25-30
Theme: Christ's invitation to take his yoke

Call to Worship

Pastor: When we consider God's laws; they seem like a heavy yoke with which we are burdened.

People: We are reminded that Jesus invited us to take his yoke, which is light and easy to bear.

Pastor: Jesus comes in fulfillment of the law, giving us grace when the law would condemn us.

People: We are burdened with sin, and come to Christ, that he may lead us into the joy of salvation.

Collect

Holy Father, whose Son has seen the burden of sin which we carry; and has offered his grace to lighten our load: Receive us with our heavy burdens, and give us rest; that we may learn from our Lord the joy of salvation. In our Savior's name we pray. Amen.

Prayer of Confession

Our Father, we know how heavy the burden of sin is. And when we read your laws, our sins become all the heavier. But your Son has come to share your grace; that we may not be burdened without hope. Forgive us, God, not only for our sins we carry; but for neglecting the grace of your Son which would relieve us. Lead us into the paths of righteousness, guided by the loving grace of our Lord, that we may find your promised rest. We pray in Jesus' name. Amen.

Hymns

"How Happy Every Child of Grace"
"I Heard the Voice of Jesus Say"
"Jesus, the Sinner's Friend"
"Peace, Perfect Peace"

PROPER 10
Sunday between July 10 and 16 inclusive

First Lesson: Exodus 2:11-22
Theme: Always under God's care

Call to Worship
Pastor: We worship a God who is always present, no matter where we are.

People: Many times we are not sure what life has in store for us, but we trust God to make his will known.

Pastor: God will never abandon us, even when we feel we have left him.

People: Thanks be to God who is the author of our life!

Collect
Almighty God, who always knows where we are in the wandering of our lives: Assure us of your presence in all our life situations; that we may yield ourselves to your purpose, and fulfill your will for our lives. In Jesus' name we pray. Amen.

Prayer of Confession
Life gives us many strange feelings Lord. Sometimes we feel like a stranger; sometimes all alone. We have even doubted if you know how we feel, or care how we feel. Forgive us when we run away from you like that. Help us to be aware of your presence in our lives at all times, and to be submissive to your will as you reveal it to us. In the name of Christ, we pray. Amen.

Hymns
"Be Not Dismayed"
"God Moves in a Mysterious Way"
"He Leadeth Me: O Blessed Thought"
"If Thou But Suffer God to Guide Thee"

PROPER 10
Sunday between July 10 and 16 inclusive

Second Lesson: Romans 8:9-17
Theme: Live by the Spirit

Call to Worship
Pastor: Throughout life we must struggle with the conflict between our human nature and God's Spirit.

People: We want to live by God's Spirit, but our human nature has such strong control over us.

Pastor: If we live according to our human nature, we end in death; but if we live by God's Spirit, we are raised from death to life.

People: May God's Spirit enable us to put to death our sinful ways; that we may live with him.

Collect
Eternal God, you have given your Spirit to defend us against the power of sin. Give us the desire to live by your Spirit; that we may resist the influence of our human nature, and live as your children. In our Savior's name we pray. Amen.

Prayer of Confession
We struggle everyday, Lord, with our human nature that puts us in conflict with your Spirit. But we want to be led by your Spirit, and be your children. Forgive our weak response to the influence of your Spirit. Take possession of our wills; that we may no longer live as our human nature tells us to, but as your Spirit directs. In the name of Christ we pray. Amen.

Hymns
"Be Thou My Vision"
"Breathe on Me, Breath of God"
"Holy Spirit, Truth Divine"
"Spirit of God, Descend Upon My Heart"

PROPER 10
Sunday between July 10 and 16 inclusive

Gospel: Matthew 13:1-9, 18-23
Theme: Parable of the sower

Call to Worship

Pastor: Sin is always at work to counteract the good news of Christ.

People: But thanks be to God, the church is always at work, too! And we are glad to be a part of it.

Pastor: Amen! No matter how ineffective our efforts may seem, there is always fertile soil which bears fruit for our labors.

People: We will continue to sow the seed of faith, convinced that many will be receptive, and come into our Lord's kingdom.

Collect

Eternal God, whose kingdom continues to grow in spite of the threat of sin: Encourage us in our ministry, that we may overcome discouragement by confidence in your power at work through your church. We pray in Jesus' name. Amen.

Prayer of Confession

We are easily discouraged, Father, when we look back a few years and see how the church used to be the center of community life. We feel the church today is on the other edge of existence for many people, and defeat haunts our aspirations. Forgive us for submitting to such hopelessness, when Christ has assured us of victory. Lead us through our barren valley of depression to the fertile soil where hearts are waiting to be won to Christ our Savior, through whom we pray. Amen.

Hymns

"Am I a Soldier of the Cross"
"Christian, Dost Thou See Them"
"Fight the Good Fight"
"March On, O Soul with Strength"

PROPER 11
Sunday between July 17 and 23 inclusive

First Lesson: Exodus 3:1-12
Theme: God's revelation, a call to service

Call to Worship

Pastor: God reveals himself many times, many ways, that we may know him better.

People: Even though there is much we do not know about God; there is much we do know because he comes to each generation revealing his true nature.

Pastor: When God reveals himself, he not only shows us what he is like, but what he want us to do.

People: May we always be ready for God's visitation; that seeing him, we may hear his call to service.

Collect

Eternal God, whose self-revelation is a call to service: Make yourself known to us in our daily lives; that we may know your will for us, and respond obediently to your call. In Jesus' name we pray. Amen.

Prayer of Confession

We often complain, O God, of all that we do not understand about you. What little we do know compels us to surrender ourselves to be in your service. But we excuse ourselves because we think we don't know enough. Forgive us when we turn our backs on the burning bush, and turn deaf ears to your call to service. Reveal your will to us, and send us forth in your service; that we may be your servants of deliverance in our world today. In our Savior's name we pray. Amen.

Hymns

"Immortal, Invisibile, God Only Wise"
"Lord, Speak to Me"
"Thanks to God Whose Word Was Spoken"
"The Voice of God is Calling"

PROPER 11
Sunday between July 17 and 23 inclusive

Second Lesson: Romans 8:18-25
Theme: The great expectation

Call to Worship
Pastor: We sometimes feel that life gives us more than our share of problems.

People: There are always others who are worse off than we are; but we still tend to feel sorry for ourselves.

Pastor: The suffering of this world is quite insignificant compared to the glory we look forward to with Christ.

People: We anxiously await God's wonderful revelation when he calls us into eternity!

Collect
Almighty and most wonderful Father, who has promised through your Son that a wonderful future is our hope: Give us patience with the trials and tribulations of this life; that we may be constant in our faith, and sure of the hope that awaits us. We pray through Christ our Lord. Amen.

Prayer of Confession
We long to be free, Father; but we feel our sin imprisons us against our will. Our frustration leads to anxiety; and our anxiety leads us away from the hope you have promised us. Forgive us for our sins which bring so much misery, destroying the hope that is in us. Set our minds on the fact of our future glory which Christ has made available to us. In his name we pray. Amen.

Hymns
"God of Our Life"
"God of the Ages, by Whose Hand"
"My Hope is Built"
"O God, Our Help in Ages Past"

PROPER 11
Sunday between July 17 and 23 inclusive

Gospel: Matthew 13:24-30, 36-43
Theme: Parable of the weeds

Call to Worship

Pastor: Our Lord's church is flesh and blood — people who are working to bring his Kingdom on earth.

People: Some people in the church do not seem to be much concerned about being Christians.

Pastor: Some may not be Christians. But God will deal with them in his own way, in his own time.

People: May God help us be true Christians; so we can help, rather than hinder, the ministry of his church.

Collect

Almighty God, who, in the Final Day, will separate non-believers from those committed to Christ: Free us from our desire to judge one another, and make us faithful in your service, that we may be forever in your Kingdom with our Savior, through whom we pray. Amen.

Prayer of Confession

Father, your church is made up of sinners saved by grace, as well as sinners unconcerned about grace. That disturbs us, and makes us want to cleanse your church of its impurities. But none of us is perfect, and none of us has the right to exclude others. Forgive us for our ambitious judgment which competes with your authority, and cripples the ministry of your church. Help us to be sincere in our faith, and in our service, regardless of the insincerity of others in your church. We pray through Christ our Lord. Amen.

Hymns

"A Charge to Keep I Have"
"God Send Us Men"
"Jesus Calls Us"
"O For a Faith that Will Not Shrink"

PROPER 12
Sunday between July 24 and 30 inclusive

First Lesson: Exodus 3:13-20
Theme: God, the Deliverer

Call to Worship
Pastor: We worship a God who intervenes in history to deliver his people.

People: God did a mighty thing when he called Moses to deliver the Israelites from Egypt.

Pastor: The God who revealed himself through Moses is the same God who has revealed himself to us through his Son.

People: We praise God for our deliverance from sin, and hope of sharing in his kingdom.

Collect
Most gracious God, you always know where your people are, and come to their rescue! Give us clear minds and open hearts to know who you are; that we may find that promised rest in the security of your love which you have revealed through your Son, our Savior. In his name we pray. Amen.

Prayer of Confession
We question life so often, God, and wonder why things are as they are. In our doubts, we often become blind to your revelation in Christ, and the deliverance he gives. Forgive us when we grope in despair, unable to see what you are trying to show us. Be Our Deliverer, and rescue us from our slavery to sin; that we may come alive to praise and serve you. In our Savior's name we pray. Amen.

Hymns
"God of Our Life"
"Guide Me, O Thou Great Jehovah"
"How Great Thou Art"
"O Lord, Our Fathers Oft Have Told"

PROPER 12
Sunday between July 24 and 30 inclusive

Second Lesson: Romans 8:26-30
Theme: God's Spirit enables us to pray

Call to Worship
Pastor: Prayer is communion with God; but sometimes we do not know how to express our feelings to God.

People: We still pray to God, even if it is feelings only, without words.

Pastor: That is because God's Spirit comes to us in prayer, and communicates to God with words we are unable to express.

People: We praise God for his Spirit which intercedes on our behalf!

Collect
Gracious Father, whose Spirit joins us in our prayers, enabling us to share our deepest feelings with you: Make us sensitive to the presence of your Spirit as we pray, that we may be honest and sincere in the sharing of our souls with you. Hear us through Christ our Lord. Amen.

Prayer of Confession
We believe in prayer, Father, but we feel inadequate, and inexperienced. We are frustrated with not knowing how to say what we feel; and so we pray too little. Forgive us for not depending more on your Spirit to support us in our prayers. Keep us in the spirit of prayer; that we may have better communion with you, and receive the strength which you provide through prayer. In our Savior's name we pray. Amen.

Hymns
"Blessed Jesus, at Thy Word"
"O Gracious Father of Mankind"
"Prayer Is the Soul's Sincere Desire"
"Sweet Hour of Prayer"

PROPER 12
Sunday between July 24 and 30 inclusive

Gospel: Matthew 13:44-52
Theme: Parables of the Kingdom

Call to Worship

Pastor: No greater value can be placed on anything than the Kingdom of Heaven. And it is offered to each of us!

People: There is no comparison of God's Kingdom with anything of earthly value.

Pastor: But if we value earthly things too much, we may lose the Kingdom. The choice is ours.

People: We want more than anything in the world to be in God's Kingdom. May God help us keep our priorities in order.

Collect

O God our Father: You have put within our reach the blessings of your Kingdom, more valuable than our minds can comprehend! Give us the wisdom to keep all our possessions and desires subordinate to your Kingdom; that we may receive the blessings inherent in your Kingdom. In our Savior's name we pray. Amen.

Prayer of Confession

We are obsessed with being accepted into your Kingdom, Father. But we also enjoy the fine pleasures and possessions of this world. Forgive us when we take for granted our entrance into your Kingdom while we invest in this world's attractions. Convince us of the choice we must make of surrendering all for the sake of your Kingdom; that we may not be led astray, thinking we can have the best of two worlds. We pray through Christ our Lord. Amen.

Hymns

"Be Thou My Vision"
"Come, Thou Almighty King"
"Take My Life, and Let It Be Consecrated"

PROPER 13
Sunday between July 31 and August 6 inclusive

First Lesson: Exodus 12:1-14
Theme: Celebrate God's redemptive acts in history

Call to Worship
Pastor: History is full of evidence that God has been real to his people.
People: We rejoice in our faith heritage which witnesses to a God who saves his people.
Pastor: From the first Passover to the Last Supper, we are reminded that God is our Deliverer. The blood of the Lamb is the mark of our salvation.
People: We celebrate with thanksgiving, the assurance we have that God will most certainly bring us into his glory forever and ever! Amen.

Collect
Gracious God, by your hand you delivered the Israelites out of Egypt. By the death of your Son, you deliver us out of the power of sin. Come to us now as we remember these great events, and mark us as people of your Kingdom now and forever; that we may celebrate these great acts in history as symbols of our own deliverance. In our Savior's name we pray. Amen.

Confession
Forgive us, O God, when we remember the redemptive acts of your mercy without identifying with the redemption they represent. Deliver us from the sins which enslave us; that we may be free to celebrate the power of your love, and rejoice in your salvation. In Jesus' name we pray. Amen.

Hymns
"Amazing Grace!"
"O My Soul, Bless God the Father"
"Pass Me Not, O Gentle Savior"
"What Wondrous Love Is This"

PROPER 13
Sunday between July 31 and August 6 inclusive

Second Lesson: Romans 8:31-39
Theme: Christ makes us victorious

Call to Worship
Pastor: God's love is a permanent gift which can never be taken from us.

People: Jesus has made that love forever ours through his death on the cross.

Pastor: There are still strong powers of evil in our world; but they cannot separate us from God's love.

People: We are certain that God gives us victory over all these powers, keeping us in his love through Christ Jesus our Lord!

Collect
Almighty God, whose love in Christ can never be taken away from us by any worldly power: Deepen our faith in Christ, that his victory on the cross may become our victory over sin and evil. In our Savior's name we pray. Amen.

Prayer of Confession
We do not believe, Father, that the Christian Faith is a mental escape from the reality of sin, or death, or any other evil force. But while we know these powers are real we still fail to experience the victory of Christ which keeps us secure in your love. Forgive us for our spiritual weakness when we have ignored the power of Christ in our lives. Show us the victory which is ours in Christ, that we may live in the strength of your love forever. We pray in Jesus' name. Amen.

Hymns
"Jesus, Thine All-Victorious Love"
"Love Divine, All Loves Excelling"
"O Love Divine, How Sweet Thou Art"
"O Love That Wilt Not Let Me Go"

PROPER 13
Sunday between July 31 and August 6 inclusive

Gospel: Matthew 14:13-21
Theme: Jesus feeds the five thousand

Call to Worship
Pastor: The feeding of the five thousand illustrates Jesus' willingness, and ability, to satisfy man's hunger.
People: The hunger we experience in our souls is also satisfied by our Lord.
Pastor: Jesus' disciples helped him feed the crowd. And Jesus needs his church today to help satisfy our world's deepest hunger.
People: We give ourselves to our Lord to share in his ministry to our world.

Collect
Heavenly Father, whose Son is unlimited in his ability to satisfy our needs: Give us receptive hearts to his ministry on our behalf; and use us in his ministry to serve others who hunger for his Word. Thus may our world know the satisfaction of feeding on our Savior's love. In his name we pray. Amen.

Prayer of Confession
Dear Father, we know the satisfaction of being nurtured by your Son. But we still go astray, only to find our hunger unsatisfied. Forgive us when we have walked away even as you invite us to partake of your blessings. Forgive us, too, for our failure to be in ministry, sharing your blessings with others. Feed us, Lord, till we want no more, and then send us forth to share our overflowing blessings with others. We pray in our Savior's name. Amen.

Hymns
"Bread of the World"
"Break Thou the Bread of Life"
"Come, Sinners, to the Gospel Feast"
"Guide Me, O Thou Great Jehovah"

PROPER 14
Sunday between August 7 and 13 inclusive

First Lesson: Exodus 14:19-31
Theme: God's protective love

Call to Worship

Pastor: As we journey through life, we cannot avoid the threat of fear and danger.

People: Everyday we are reminded that life is uncertain and on the edge of destruction.

Pastor: But God is certain to be with us to remove the fear, and overcome the danger.

People: Yes, God always makes a way for us to march forward with joy, singing his praises!

Collect

Almighty God, who guides us through the difficulties in life with the certainty of your presence and protection: Grant us peace and solitude with the assurance that life with its stress, cannot defeat the power of your love. Thus may we journey through life focusing our energies on following you, undaunted by the empty threats of a temporal world. In Christ's name we pray. Amen.

Prayer of Confession

Forgive us, O God, when we let fear blind us to your hand leading us through life. Grant us the faith and commitment to trust you for direction and protection; that we may experience the joy of living in the shelter of your protective love. Hear us for Jesus' sake. Amen.

HYMNS

"A Mighty Fortress Is Our God"
"Captain of Israel's Host"
"Give to the Winds Thy Fears"
"God of Our Life"

PROPER 14
Sunday between August 7 and 13 inclusive
Second Lesson: Romans 9:1-5
Theme: A concern for Jews to accept Jesus

Call to Worship
Pastor: Jesus was born a Jew in the flesh, but many Jews did not receive him as Savior.

People: The are still God's children, and are therefore to be included in God's plan of salvation.

Pastor: We share Paul's concern for them, and cannot exclude them from God's love; nor can we cease to pray for their salvation.

People: We pray that all descendants of Abraham may accept the love of God in Jesus Christ.

Collect
O loving Father, whose love for your chosen race is still the source of their salvation: Grant us the mercy and the compassion to pray for all your children to be included in your church; that your name may be praised by all, through your Son Jesus the Christ, in whose name we pray. Amen.

Prayer of Confession
Father, we know those of the Jewish Faith believe in you without regard to Jesus as Savior. But we are confused about our relationship with them. Forgive us when we have either considered them saved without Christ, or else unsavable because of their errors. Renew us in a mission of compassion and concern; that your love for them may yet bring them salvation. In our Savior's name we pray. Amen.

Hymns
"Christ Is the World's True Light"
"Heralds of Christ"
"The Church's One Foundation"
"Ye Servants of God"

PROPER 14
Sunday between August 7 and 13 inclusive

Gospel: Matthew 14:22-33
Theme: Jesus walks on the water

Call to Worship

Pastor: Our mission as the church is often like a ship, tossed on the sea.

People: Church history has recorded many storms; but Christ always brings a calm, encouraging his followers.

Pastor: We have our bouts with fear and discouragement, too. But we can be sure our Lord will see us through.

People: We worship Jesus, the Son of God who is with us in all our struggles, bringing peace to our souls.

Collect

Father of grace and power, whose Son gives victory over life's most violent storms: Strengthen our faith as we commit ourselves to the ministry of your church; that we may be secure in our relationship with you, and true to our mission in our world. We pray through Christ our Lord. Amen.

Prayer of Confession

We love your church, Father, because we enjoy its security in a life of insecurity. But even within your church we experience fear when we give thought to the tremendous forces which sweep over us as if we were defenseless. Forgive us when we have surrendered our faith to the forces of evil. Keep us mindful of your presence and power, that we may rejoice with you in the victory of your church. We pray through Christ our Lord. Amen.

Hymns

"Father, I Stretch My Hands to Thee"
"Jesus, My Strength, My Hope"
"O For a Faith that Will No Shrink"
"The Church's One Foundation"

PROPER 15
Sunday between August 14 and 20 inclusive

First Lesson: Exodus 16:2-15
Theme: God feeds the Israelites in the wilderness

Call to Worship

Pastor: God is here. And he knows the anxiety we experience when we are troubled or frightened.

People: God loves us, even when we are impatient, and provides for our needs.

Pastor: Let us lift our hearts in praise to God for the wonderful ways in which he blesses us.

People: Great is our God in whom we put our trust. He does not leave us, or forsake us!

Collect

Almighty God, who provides for our needs even though we worry and complain: Strengthen our faith in your providence, that we may live in the assurance that you will care for us and meet all our needs. In Jesus' name we pray. Amen.

Prayer of Confession

You have never deserted us, Father, yet when trouble arises, we are quick to worry or become afraid. Sometimes we blame you, and ask why. Forgive us for not giving you our trust, believing that you know our need and will provide for us. Remind us of all the wonderful acts you have performed for your people, that wemay know we have nothing to fear with you being our God. We pray through Christ our Lord. Amen.

Hymns

"O Lord, Our Fathers Oft Have Told"
"Praise to the Lord, the Almighty"
"Through All the Changing Scenes of Life"
"Unto the Hills I lift Mine Eyes"

PROPER 15
Sunday between August 14 and 20 inclusive

Second Lesson: Romans 11:13-16, 29-32
Theme: God's mercy for the disobedient

Call to Worship

Pastor: God has made his love available to all people in hopes they will accept salvation.

People: We are all guilty of disobedience, and deserve to be rejected by God; yet he shows mercy instead.

Pastor: When God offers his love, he does not change his mind and retract it.

People: We have seen God's mercy in his love for us. We bless him for our salvation!

Collect

Merciful Father, who is unwilling to call back your love you have given: Forgive our disobedience, and be merciful to us; that we may be redeemed to new life through Jesus Christ, Our Lord, in whose name we pray. Amen.

Prayer of Confession

Dear Father, we come to you as disobedient children who have betrayed your love. Our sins make us unworthy to call you Father. But you have promised mercy, and so we ask for your forgiveness, believing you will reclaim us as your children. Strengthen us in our discipleship, that our witness may convince others your mercy is sufficient to restore them. We pray through Christ our Redeemer. Amen.

Hymns

"Amazing Grace"
"Depth of Mercy"
"Heavenly Father, Bless Me Now"
"There's a Wideness in God's Mercy"

PROPER 15
Sunday between August 14 and 20 inclusive

Gospel: Matthew 15:21-28
Theme: The Canaanite woman's faith

Call to Worship
Pastor: Many barriers come between God and his people, limiting his ability to give wholeness.

People: It seemed the Canaanite woman would be rejected; but her faith overcame her barriers, and brought healing to her daughter.

Pastor: The gift of faith is available to everyone, and breaks through any barrier to God's grace.

People: May God give us faith to overcome any obstacle which seems to withhold his love from us.

Collect
Father of love and mercy, whose blessings come in proportion to our faith: Make firm our faith in your redemptive grace for all people; and break down every barrier which would keep us from your love; that we may find healing for our souls. We pray in our Savior's name. Amen.

Prayer of Confession
Sometimes, Father, it seems we just cannot get through to you. It may be guilt, or fear, or sometimes a feeling of unworthiness. But our separation is more than we can stand; and we need to know you accept us. Forgive us for the barriers we create; and forgive us for too little faith to overcome these barriers. Restore our faith in your Son, our Savior, that he may come into our lives with the assurance of our being made whole. In his name we pray. Amen.

Hymns
"Come, Every Soul by Sin Oppressed"
"Father, I Stretch My Hands to Thee"
"My Faith Looks Up to Thee"
"Pass Me Not, O Gentle Savior"

PROPER 16
Sunday between August 21 and 27 inclusive

First Lesson: Exodus 17:1-7
Theme: Anxiety eased by Christ's presence

Call to Worship
Pastor: Have you ever felt left by God to struggle alone with your problems?

People: Our faith tells us God never leaves us. But fear often makes us feel stranded in our anxiety.

Pastor: When we feel that way, we need to focus on the promise and presence of Christ who refreshes our souls with hope.

People: Life may seem like a dry and thirsty land; but thanks be to God for the thirst-quenching of his Son, our Savior!

Collect
Almighty God, whose Son is the source of life: Come to us in our end of the rope experiences with the awareness of our Savior's presence; that we may discover our needs are met when we put our faith in him. In his name we pray. Amen.

Prayer of Confession
We panic easily, Lord, when we feel life is overcome with threats. Forgive us when we blame you for our painful experiences, instead of depending on you to heal our pain. Increase our faith to rest in the assurance of your love; that we may know the joy of our Savior's company. In his name we pray. Amen.

Hymns
"Come, Thou Fount of Every Blessing"
"God of the Ages, by Whose Hand"
"Guide Me, O Thou Great Jehovah"
"Lead Us, O Father"

PROPER 16
Sunday between August 21 and 27 inclusive

Second Lesson: Romans 11:33-36
Theme: A doxology to God

Call to Worship

Pastor: How wonderful is our God! His glory exceeds the greatest praise of our lips!

People: We bless the Lord our God with heart, mind, and soul; and still we feel we have hardly begun to praise his name!

Pastor: We have reached deep into space, and yet have only scratched the surface of his creative works!

People: All praise and honor be to God. To him be the glory forever!

Collect

Almighty and most merciful God: You have shared the riches of your glory both through the natural order of creation and through the spiritual order of salvation. Accept our worship we give to you in honor of your great wisdom and unlimited love. Thus may we witness to our redemption through your Son Jesus, our Lord, in whose name we pray. Amen.

Prayer of Confession

Heavenly Father, in humility and in penitence we bow before you. Our lives are nothing but a blot on the beauty of your wonderful acts, in history. You have made us in your image; yet we have marred your likeness so that there is little resemblance. Forgive us, Father, for crawling in sin, when you would raise us in glory. Unleash your mighty love and power upon us, and restore us to fellowship with you. We pray through Christ our Lord. Amen.

Hymns

"All Creatures of Our God and King"
"I Sing the Almighty Power of God"
"Joyful, Joyful, We adore Thee"
"O How Glorious, Full of Wonder"

PROPER 16
Sunday between August 21 and 27 inclusive

Gospel: Matthew 16.13-20
Theme: Peter declares Jesus to be the Messiah

Call to Worship

Pastor: Many questions were raised as to who Jesus was. Even his disciples had different answers.

People: Peter knew Jesus was the Messiah, the Son of the living God!

Pastor: It was by faith in God's revelation that Peter could say that. That same faith can be ours.

People: We do believe Jesus is the Son of God, our Savior! May our faith add to the strengthening of his church.

Collect

Eternal Father, who reveals the divinity of your Son to those who are receptive to faith: Give us such faith to know your Son as Savior; that we may build, with strong conviction, your church in our world. In our Savior's name we pray. Amen.

Prayer of Confession

There is no doubt in our minds, Father, that Jesus is your Son. And the church is his witness in our world today. But faith so easily becomes impersonal theology; and we fail to be builders of a church which stands against the forces of evil. Forgive us for our unstable ways which we consider to be discipleship. Help us to make our faith vital, and personal, that your church may be able to depend on our witness. We pray through Christ our Lord. Amen.

Hymns

"Ask Ye What Great Thing I Know"
"Author of Faith, Eternal Word"
"Strong Son of God, Immortal Love"
"The Church's One Foundation"

PROPER 17
Sunday between August 28 and September 3 inclusive

First Lesson: Exodus 19:1-9
Theme: God's call to be holy

Call to Worship
Pastor: All creation belongs to God, and all people.
People: But many people do not know God; and many others do not love him as they ought.
Pastor: Many reject or ignore God, because he calls his people to live holy lives.
People: We do not want to be self-righteous. But we desire to be more holy in accordance with God's will.

Collect
Holy Father, who calls your children to be holy: Give us the inspiration of your Spirit; that we may order our lives after your will, and aim to be holy in all our endeavors. We pray through Christ our Lord. Amen.

Prayer of Confession
We talk about being a Christian nation, Father, but we are far from being holy. We are too satisfied with a few statistics which reflect the presence of your church. Forgive us, who have received so much of your bounty, for not hearing and answering your call to live as a holy nation. Guide us, and all who are a part of your church, into the life which brings wholeness, not only to individuals, but to nations as well. We pray in Jesus' name. Amen.

Hymns
"God, Who Touchest Earth with Beauty"
"Holy Spirit, Truth Divine"
"I Need Thee Every Hour"
"Take Time to Be Holy"

PROPER 17
Sunday between August 28 and September 3 inclusive

Second Lesson: Romans 12:1-13
Theme: Be a living sacrifice to God

Call to Worship
Pastor: God has made salvation possible through his Son, Jesus, our Lord and Savior.

People: Because of God's love in Christ, we owe God the best lives that we can live.

Pastor: We should live as persons transformed by God's love, instead of being conformed to the ways of the world.

People: May our true worship of God be our daily lives, lived to his honor and glory.

Collect
Most gracious Father, whose wondrous love has restored us to life when our sins would claim us for death's victory: Enable us to offer ourselves to you as a living sacrifice, that we may be transformed by your Spirit in defiance of the world's persuasion to conform. Hear us for Jesus' sake. Amen.

Prayer of Confession
Hear us, Father, as we beg your forgiveness for the poor worship our daily lives have expressed. We want to be transformed by your Spirit; but the power of the world is great, and we cannot resist. Let Jesus come into our hearts and cleanse us from within; that we may grow in your grace, and offer you true devotion. In our Savior's name we pray. Amen.

Hymns
"Have Thine Own Way, Lord"
"I Am Thine, O Lord"
"O Jesus, I Have Promised"
"Take My Life, and Let It Be Consecrated"

PROPER 17
Sunday between August 28 and September 3 inclusive

Gospel: Matthew 16:21-28
Theme: Discipleship demands self-denial

Call to Worship

Pastor: To live the Christian life is to put Christ first, even above self.

People: Putting the Christian life first often leads to cross-bearing on his behalf.

Pastor: We may feel we have sacrificed our life; but in that sacrifice, we find real life.

People: We desire to commit ourselves wholly to the Lord; assured that he will bless us with abundant living!

Collect

Almighty God, whose Son calls disciples who are willing to lay aside personal values for commitment to him: Convince us that living for our own selfish ends is a losing investment, that we may forget ourselves in your service and experience the joy of living for you. In Jesus' name we pray. Amen.

Prayer of Confession

We enjoy life, Father, but much of our joy is superficial because we strive to please ourselves. Forgive us for not seeing life as a gift we can give to you. Challenge us with the discipleship our Lord requires; that we may not only be effective in service to him, but also find the life that is most satisfying to us. We pray through Christ our Lord. Amen.

Hymns

"Am I a Soldier of the Cross"
"Jesus, I My Cross Have Taken"
"Must Jesus Bear the Cross Alone"
"Take Up Thy Cross"

PROPER 18
Sunday between September 4 and 10 inclusive

First Lesson: Exodus 19:16-24
Theme: The glory, majesty, and power of God

Call to Worship

Pastor: Holy is our God who created heaven and earth. His glory fills the universe!

People: He is awesome in glory, majesty, and power; and is worthy of our devotion.

Pastor: We stand in awe of him, because he alone is God. There is none like him.

People: We worship God, who though he became flesh like us, is beyond the reach of our greatest potential.

Collect

Almighty God, your power is beyond our comprehension; your majesty overwhelms our imagination; and your glory exceeds our understanding! Nevertheless, we bow in awe before you believing you have claimed us as your children whom you love, and for whom you sent your Son to rescue from sin. In his name we pray. Amen.

Prayer of Confession

We do not challenge your greatness, O God. But often we deny it by acting more like buddies than servants. Forgive us when we ignore the majesty of your divine nature. Grant us submissive hearts to your authority, that we may find redemption in the security of your power, and discover our reason for being. In our Savior's name we pray. Amen.

Hymns

"Before Jehovah's Awful Throne"
"Holy, Holy, Holy!"
"O Worship the King"
"The Lord Jehovah Reigns"

PROPER 18
Sunday between September 4 and 10 inclusive

Second Lesson: Romans 13:1-10
Theme: Let love be sincere

Call to Worship
Pastor: God's love is genuine and self-giving. He expects our love for one another to be just as real.
People: We are brothers and sisters in Christ, and need to share our faith and love with each other.
Pastor: Our love should also be just as real for those who abuse us; for they too, are God's children.
People: May our lives become instruments of God whereby he can bring peace and joy to our world.

Collect
Eternal God, our heavenly Father, who loves us even when we are unlovable: Grant us the desire and ability to love one another with sincerity, that the example of your children may usher in the day of peace and brotherhood. We pray through Christ our Lord. Amen.

Prayer of Confession
Dear Father, we know our high calling is to love; and we do profess our love. Yet within our hearts is the same spirit that produces hate and hurt. Forgive us for love which flows from our tongue, but not from our hearts. Wash out the carnal nature of our hearts which makes us warriors instead of peacemakers; that we may be persons who love, rather than lie. In Jesus' name we pray. Amen.

Hymns
"All Praise to Our Redeeming Lord"
"Blest Be the Dear Uniting Love"
"Jesus, United by Thy Grace"
"O Brother Man, Fold to Thy Heart"

PROPER 18
Sunday between September 4 and 10 inclusive

Gospel: Matthew 18:15-20
Theme: The church's responsibility to sinners

Call to Worship
Pastor: We are persons with human nature. And therefore we sin against each other from time to time.

People: It is difficult to relate to persons when they offend or abuse us.

Pastor: But our Christian duty is to go to them in love, showing how they have hurt us.

People: May God help us to be that honest with one another, giving strength to our Christian fellowship.

Collect
Father in heaven, who directs your church to be a corrective enabler, when we sin against one another: Give us compassion and genuine love toward those who hurt us; that we may enable them to understand their errors and correct them. We pray through Christ our Lord. Amen.

Prayer of Confession
We are human, Father, and therefore, we hurt when Christian friends offend us. And in our hurt, we become angry toward them, instead of concerned for them. Forgive us when we have not come face to face with them in the conflict, with a desire to restore wholeness in the church. Help us to love one another enough to be honest with each other when sin tries to ruin our fellowship. Grant us your Spirit, both to sinners and to those who are sinned against. We pray in Jesus' name. Amen.

Hymns
"Jesus, We Look to Thee"
"Jesus, with Thy Church Abide"
"O Brother Man, Fold to Thy Heart"
"When We Walk with the Lord"

PROPER 19
Sunday between September 11 and 17 inclusive

First Lesson: Exodus 20:1-20
Theme: Rules for the redeemed

Call to Worship
Pastor: God is love, but his love requires the obedience of those he loves.
People: We depend on God's love, but we also depend on his laws.
Pastor: That's right. His laws are given that we might enjoy life at it's best.
People: May we be as receptive to God's laws as we are to his love; and live in accordance with his will.

Collect
Eternal God, you have set us free to be your obedient children. Quicken us to obey your commands, and live in harmony with your will; that we may enjoy the blessings of life according to your design. In Jesus' name we pray. Amen.

Prayer of Confession
Your laws are necessary, O God, for us to live with one another, and with you. But we take them lightly as we rewrite our own guidelines for living. Forgive us when we claim your love, but reject your laws. Instill your laws in our minds, and write them in our hearts; that we may experience the life for which your love has redeemed us. In our Savior's name we pray. Amen.

Hymns
"Come, Thou Almighty King"
"Have Thine Own Way, Lord"
"How Gentle God's Commands"
"When We Walk with the Lord"

PROPER 19
Sunday between September 11 and 17 inclusive

Second Lesson: Romans 14:5-12
Theme: Our convictions should honor God

Call to Worship

Pastor: God has cleansed us of sin, and raised us to new life through his Son, Jesus our Lord.

People: Because of our faith in Christ we serve God by living according to our convictions.

Pastor: Our convictions may differ from one another; but we must be sure that they give honor to God, not to ourselves.

People: Our lives belong to Jesus, who saved us from the power of sin. Honor and glory be to him!

Collect

Gracious Father, who has lifted us from the depth of sin by the love of Jesus: Unite us in our affirmations of faith; that we may use our convictions to speak in a united voice, giving honor to your great name. We pray through Christ our Lord. Amen.

Prayer of Confession

We belong to one church, Father; but we interpret discipleship in different ways, resulting in a variety of convictions. We hurt, rather than help one another as we defend our differences. Forgive us for the fractures we cause, when we ought to bring healing and wholeness to your church. Help us to bind ourselves together in Christian love supporting each other in faith and practice. In Jesus' name we pray. Amen.

Hymns

"At Length There Dawns the Glorious Day"
"God Send Us Men"
"Lord, Speak to Me"
"O For a Faith That Will Not Shrink"

PROPER 19
Sunday between September 11 and 17 inclusive

Gospel: Matthew 18:21-35
Theme: The unforgiving servant

Call to Worship

Pastor: God's forgiveness is so very great when we consider how sinful we are.

People: We would be doomed for eternity if it were not for God's forgiveness.

Pastor: Jesus tells us God's forgiveness is not ours if we do not forgive those who sin against us.

People: May God help us forgive others as he forgives us.

Collect

Almighty God, who requires that we forgive those who wrong us, just as you forgive our sins: Give us the grace to forgive one another; that we may restore broken fellowships, and consummate our forgiveness in Christ, through whom we pray. Amen.

Prayer of Confession

As sinners, we depend on your forgiveness, Father. Yet it is that same sinful nature which makes us so unforgiving toward other sinners. Forgive us for holding grudges, and wishing for revenge against our adversaries, when you have been so free with your forgiveness toward us. Remove our bitterness; and fill us with love; that we may express true forgiveness to those who wrong us. In Jesus' name we pray. Amen.

Hymns

"Eternal Son, Eternal Love"
"Father Eternal, Ruler of Creation"
"God of Grace and God of Glory"
"Lift Up Our Hearts, O King of Kings"

PROPER 20
Sunday between September 18 and 24 inclusive

First Lesson: Exodus 32:1-14
Theme: God expresses mercy when we deserve wrath

Call to Worship

Pastor: Israel's sin of idolatry with the golden calf was a real test of God's mercy.

People: We are amazed when we read of God's patience with Israel during their journey to the promised land.

Pastor: His mercy with us is no less marvelous when we think of how we try his patience with our sinning.

People: We thank God for his Son who intercedes on our behalf, bringing us mercy that is greater than our sins!

Collect

O loving God, whose mercy far exceeds the limits of any love you owe to us: Withhold your anger which we deserve, that we may experience forgiveness through your Son, Jesus our Savior, who intercedes on our behalf. In his name we pray. Amen.

Prayer of Confession

We do not bow down to golden calves, Father, but our sins deny your lordship just the same. We sin against our better judgment and against your divine laws every day. Forgive us for our persistence, and the intensity with which we sin. May your mercy through Christ transform our inclination to sin into a desire to love and serve you. We pray in Jesus' name. Amen.

Hymns

"Come, Thou Fount of Every Blessing"
"Majestic Sweetness Sits Enthroned"
"There's a Wideness in God's Mercy"
"What Wondrous Love Is This?"
"When All Thy Mercies, O My God"

PROPER 20
Sunday between September 18 and 24 inclusive

Second Lesson: Philippians 1:21-27
Theme: Live as the gospel requires

Call to Worship

Pastor: The gospel of Jesus Christ is the good news of God's love.

People: Christ has come to redeem us from sin, and raise us to new life.

Pastor: Our new life in Christ should demonstrate his teachings as well as his salvation. That, too, is the gospel.

People: May our lives become the gospel of Christ, interpreting God's love to others.

Collect

Father God, who has given your only Son to teach us the godly life, and to save us from the sinful life: Make us firm in our faith, that we may live in obedience to the gospel as given by Jesus our Lord, through whom we pray. Amen.

Prayer of Confession

We claim Jesus as our Savior, Father, because the good news of his salvation has been told to us. But we have listened more to our Lord's word of redemption than to his disciplines for living. Forgive us for our life styles that do not reflect the gospel of new life in Christ. Help us to live in accordance with the gospel, that we may be faithful in our witness. We pray in our Savior's name. Amen.

Hymns

"Lord, I Want to Be a Christian"
"O Jesus, I Have Promised"
"Take Time to Be Holy"
"Take Up Thy Cross"

PROPER 20
Sunday between September 18 and 24 inclusive

Gospel: Matthew 20:1-16
Theme: The workers in the vineyard

Call to Worship

Pastor: The heavenly reward God promises to his children is not a reward we earn by good works.

People: We could never become righteous enough to make up for past sin, or to be worthy of heaven.

Pastor: God's love is given, then, not in proportion to our righteousness, but simply because he is love

People: We thank God for loving us. May we never become jealous over his love to others who may seem less deserving than ourselves.

Collect

Gracious Father, who desires to forgive all sinners when they turn to you in repentance: Rid our minds of the worldly ways in which we evaluate a person's worthiness of forgiveness, that we may know our own forgiveness is by grace alone, and not by any righteousness of ours. In our Savior's name we pray. Amen.

Prayer of Confession

Faith convinces us of your Kingdom, Father, and of our forgiveness and acceptance into your Kingdom. But when we look at other sinners who repent so late in life, we wonder why they should be included. Forgive us for thinking we have earned, or deserved, a place in your Kingdom because of our years of service. Fill our hearts with thanksgiving for a redemption which is not based on good works. We pray through Christ our Lord. Amen.

Hymns

"Amazing Grace"
"Jesus, Where'er Thy People Meet"
"There's a Wideness in God's Mercy"
"What Shall I Do My God to Love"

PROPER 21
Sunday between September 25 and October 1 inclusive

First Lesson: Exodus 33:12-23
Theme: God's loving presence

Worship
Pastor: Even though we do not know what the future holds, we do know God holds the future in his hands.

People: We are confident that God is with us as we go into the unknown of each tomorrow.

Pastor: Tomorrow will never be a threat to us. Whatever fears it may create, God will defeat them by his glorious presence.

People: We are happy knowing God is with us. We rejoice in the faith he has given us to live a victorious life.

Collect
Gracious God, whose presence is the source of hope and protection for your people: Give us the assurance of your presence in our journey through life; that we may celebrate with joy our adventure in faith, and your demonstration of love. In the name of Christ we pray. Amen.

Prayer of Confession
We know we cannot survive, O God, without your presence to nurture and protect us through life. But we still find ourselves trying to go it alone, only to increase our pain. Forgive us when we make decisions in denial of your presence, and contradict your will. Lead us in the lifestyle you would have us live; that we may enjoy life as a journey with you. In the name of Christ we pray. Amen.

Hymns
"Nearer, My God, to Thee"
"O God, Our Help in Ages Past"
"O Master, Let Me Walk with Thee"
"Pass Me Not, O Gentle Savior"

PROPER 21
Sunday between September 25 and October 1 inclusive

Second Lesson: Philippians 2:1-13
Theme: Christian fellowship: unity, love, humility

Call to Worship
Pastor: Christ our Lord united his followers together in Christian love.

People: The presence of Christ makes our fellowship a happy experience.

Pastor: When Christ is our life, our fellowship takes on the nature of Christ, and we experience unity, love, and humility toward one another.

People: May Christ live in us, that we may be like him.

Collect
O holy Father, whose perfect Son became flesh to share his glory with us: Reveal to us the divine nature of your Son, that our concern for one another may reflect the example of our Savior, through whom we pray. Amen.

Prayer of Confession
Dear Father, we are followers of your Son, Jesus Christ. We gather as congregations, and are united as your church. But in our fellowship we experience too little of the nature of Christ. Forgive us for denying our Lord's presence with our petty conflicts. Transform our human nature by the nature of Christ, that your church may become a fellowship of compassion. We pray through Christ our Lord. Amen.

Hymns
"All Praise to Our Redeeming Lord"
"All Praise to Thee, for Thou O King Divine"
"Blest Be the Tie That Binds"
"God Be With You"

PROPER 21
Sunday between September 25 and October 1 inclusive

Gospel: Matthew 21:28-32
Theme: The obedient and disobedient sons

Call to Worship

Pastor: The obedience God requires is not just what we say with our mouths, but what we do with our lives.

People: Faith expressed through prayer must also be expressed through the way we live.

Pastor: God's word is clear: Sinners who repent will find God's mercy before praying people who do as they please.

People: We desire to put our faith into practice by living in obedience to God's will.

Collect

Almighty and most merciful Father, whose mercy is without end toward those who respond in obedience to your word: Convict us of our shallow faith when we profess with our lips, obedience which we are unwilling to put in practice; that we may find mercy and grace to atone for our sins. We pray in Jesus' name. Amen.

Prayer of Confession

We are very promising in our prayers, Father. But when it comes to daily life, we find reasons to postpone the fulfillment of our promises. Forgive us for saying so much, and doing so little. Inspire us to live obedient lives to your honor and glory; that your promised mercy may be fulfilled in us. In our Savior's name we pray. Amen.

Hymns

"I Want a Principle Within"
"Sinners, Turn: Why Will You Die"
"Take My Life, and Let It Be Consecrated"
"When We Walk with the Lord"

PROPER 22
Sunday between October 2 and 8 inclusive

First Lesson: Numbers 27:12-23
Theme: Joshua succeeds Moses

Call to Worship
Pastor: The church has survived the centuries, because God has raised up leaders in each generation.

People: We are all limited in the years we can give to serve our Lord. But God adds our years to those of servants before and after us; and ministry continues.

Pastor: It is important that we each hear God's call, so we will be faithful servants in our specific time and place in history.

People: We are ready to serve our Lord as he sees fit; and pray that the service we give will help convince our world of God's love.

Collect
Almighty God, you have called us to give our best in the ministry of your church. Grant us your Spirit to give us courage, wisdom, and strength; that faith and commitment may bear fruit in the service we give to our Savior, Jesus Christ, in whose name we pray. Amen.

Prayer of Confession
We know you need people who will answer your call to be servants, O God. But many times we have excused ourselves for less than acceptable reasons. Forgive us when we have shirked our duty in the ministry of your church. Move each of us to do our part in being a church which ministers to our world. In our Savior's name we pray. Amen.

Hymns
"God, Send Us Men"
"Lord, Whose Love Through Humble Service"
"The Voice of God is Calling"
"We Bear the Strain of Earthly Care"

PROPER 22
Sunday between October 2 and 8 inclusive

Second Lesson: Philippians 3:12-21
Theme: Rejoice in the Lord

Call to Worship

Pastor: Lift up your hearts in joyful praise to the Lord!
People: We lift them up in thanksgiving for all the wonderful works our Lord has done!
Pastor: Pray to God with a thankful heart, and he will fill you with the peace of Christ.
People: May the peace of Christ keep us in union with him.

Collect

Most glorious and wonderful Father: You fill our hearts with praise for renewed life in Christ Jesus your Son! Now fill our minds with meditations which are noble and true, that we may be strengthened in our union with him. In his name we pray. Amen.

Prayer of Confession

We are so blessed, Father, with goodness beyond our greatest expectations. And yet, how often we take it for granted. Forgive us when our hearts have been empty, and our lips silent, because our minds have been preoccupied with less than honorable thoughts. Cleanse our minds and our hearts with the peace of Christ, that with our whole being we will give you praise. In our Savior's name we pray. Amen.

Hymns

"How Great Thou Art"
"Praise to the Lord, the Almighty"
"Rejoice, The Lord Is King"
"Rejoice, Ye Pure in Heart"

PROPER 22
Sunday between October 2 and 8 inclusive

Gospel: Matthew 21:33-43
Theme: Parable of the tenants in the vineyard

Call to Worship
Pastor: God created the human race to love him, and be loved by him.

People: God has sent many persons to call his people into committed living.

Pastor: He even sent his only Son. But many ignore him as though life were a personal possession.

People: We have received God's blessings in abundance. May we be faithful in accepting Christ's call to live in obedient discipleship

Collect
Eternal God our Heavenly Father, who blesses us with love and life, and who asks us to surrender our lives to you: Give us receptive hearts to your Son, who came to claim us as your children, that we may enjoy your Kingdom forever. In our Savior's name we pray. Amen.

Prayer of Confession
Life is full of blessings because of your love, Father. But we become very possessive with what you share with us, and deny our responsibility to you. Forgive us when our self-centeredness keeps us from surrendering our lives to you, causing us to resist the authority of your Son over our lives. Renew our faith; that we may let Jesus be Lord of our lives, leading us in faithful service to you. In his name we pray. Amen.

Hymns
"Come, Let Us, Who in Christ Believe"
"More Love to Thee, O Christ"
"O Jesus, Thou Art Standing"
"Savior, Thy Dying Love"

PROPER 23
Sunday between October 9 and 15 inclusive

First Lesson: Deuteronomy 34:1-12
Theme: God's self-revelation through Moses' death

Call to Worship
Pastor: God's great law giver, Moses, died outside the promised land, but he enabled a nation to receive the promise he had proclaimed.

People: Before Moses died, God revealed his faithfulness to him, and showed Moses the promised land.

Pastor: Like Moses, Jesus proclaimed God's promise of new life; but he died that all might receive the fulfillment of that promise.

People: Great is our God who proved his faithfulness through Moses in the old covenant, but especially through his Son with a new covenant!

Collect
Almighty God, who revealed your faithfulness to Moses at his death: Grant us the understanding of your faithfulness as revealed through your Son, Jesus, who not only revealed your promise of salvation, but fulfilled that promise by his death on our behalf. In his name we pray. Amen.

Prayer of Confession
How much we are like the Israelites, Father, who heard Moses preach your promise of deliverance, but who resisted the fulfillment of that promise. Forgive us for our blindness that prevents us from seeing your revelation, and our stubborness that prevents us from receiving your deliverance from sin. Give us the vision to see your love in our lives, that we may know your promise fulfilled in us, through Christ our Lord. Amen.

Hymns
"All the Way My Savior Leads Me"
"He Leadeth Me: O Blessed Thought"
"Standing on the Promises"

PROPER 23
Sunday between October 9 and 15 inclusive

Second Lesson: Philippians 4:1-9
Theme: Be Joyful

Call to Worship

Pastor: Rejoice in the Lord! We enjoy our fellowship with God, because of our union with Christ Jesus.

People: The love of God fills our hearts with joy! Praise God, from whom all blessings flow!

Pastor: God's love motivates us to share our joy with one another in true happiness, and holiness.

People: We are so thankful for all that God has done for us through Christ; and for all he continues to do for us as we live in union with his Son.

Collect

God of grace and glory, you have blessed us with love beyond measure! You fill our lives with joy and happiness! Our hearts are overflowing with thanksgiving! May our faith and devotion confirm our praise; that our lives may be a doxology in honor of your Son, our Savior, in whose name we pray. Amen.

Prayer of Confession

We have the joy, Lord, down in our hearts. But sometimes we keep it buried there, instead of letting it blossom in our personalities. Forgive us when we suppress the joy you have given us, only to suffer sadness. Release the joy you have put within us; that we may show our praise for all your goodness to us. In the name of Christ we pray. Amen.

Hymns

"Joyful, Joyful, We Adore Thee"
"O Happy Day, That Fixed My Choice"
"Rejoice, the Lord is King"
"Rejoice, Ye Pure in Heart"

PROPER 23
Sunday between October 9 and 15 inclusive

Gospel: Matthew 22:1-14
Theme: Parable of the wedding feast

Call to Worship

Pastor: Jesus speaks to us through his church, inviting us into God's kingdom.

People: We are in the church because we want to be in God's kingdom.

Pastor: We may be in the church, yet fail to accept Christ's invitation into God's kingdom if our faith does not lead to action.

People: May our response to Christ be a personal commitment in which our faith and life enable God's kingdom to be our home.

Collect

Almighty God, who invites us into your kingdom through your Son, Jesus Christ: Keep us firm in our faith, that we may hear and answer our Lord's invitation to receive your blessings. In his name we pray. Amen.

Prayer of Confession

Father, we feel it is necessary to be in the church. But once we are in the church, we too easily become deaf to your call to Christian commitment. And in our deafness, we lose interest in Christ's invitation into your kingdom. Forgive us for the apathy we express toward the eternal blessing you share with us through Christ. Help us to be ready, willing, and excited about your promised kingdom. We pray through Christ our Lord. Amen.

Hymns

"Come, Sinners, to the Gospel Feast"
"Jesus Calls Us O'er the Tumult"
"Jesus Is Tenderly Calling"
"Sinners, Turn: Why Will You Die"

PROPER 24
Sunday between October 16 and 22 inclusive

First Lesson: Ruth 1:1-19a
Theme: Love within the family

Call to Worship
Pastor: In wisdom, God has created us to live in families, where we thrive on one another's love.

People: Without the bond of family love, we are incomplete, and do not experience the joy of wholeness.

Pastor: We rejoice in that wholeness, only when we give ourselves in total commitment to the rest of the family.

People: May our commitment be such, that life and death, joy and sorrow, faith and love, may be a mutual sharing within our families!

Collect
Gracious Father, who has created the family to be a source of identity and wholeness through the sharing of mutual love: Strengthen our families with sincere love and unity among all members, that we may experience the true joy of being your children. In the name of Christ we pray. Amen.

Prayer of Confession
With gratitude, we express our praise to you, O God, for the blessing of family ties. But so often we want to receive from the family more than we contribute. Forgive us when our selfish ways hinder the wholeness which you intend each family member to achieve. Help us so to love, that our lives will be a source of joy in our homes. In Jesus' name we pray. Amen.

Hymns
"Children of the Heavenly Father"
"Happy the Home when God Is There"
"Lord of Life and King of Glory"
"O Lord, May Church and Home Combine"

PROPER 24
Sunday between October 16 and 22 inclusive

Second Lesson: 1 Thessalonians 1:1-10
Theme: The committed life

Call to Worship

Pastor: To live the Christian life is to put your faith into practice through your life style.

People: To live the Christian life is to make love a reality in your attitude toward others.

Pastor: To live the Christian life is to stand firm in the Christian hope.

People: May God fill us with his Spirit, enabling us to live the Christian life!

Collect

Gracious Father, who has called us in love to be your children: Inspire us with your Spirit; that we may be strong in our convictions to live the Christian life. We pray through Christ our Lord. Amen.

Prayer of Confession

Our intent is to be Christian, Father; but our commitment to live the Christian life is not true to our intentions. We practice what we see more than what we say. Forgive us for our failure to demonstrate our convictions through our life style. Strengthen us by your Spirit; that our faith, hope, and love may determine the way we live. In our Savior's name we pray. Amen.

Hymns

"My Hope Is Built"
"O For a Faith that Will Not Shrink"
"O Jesus, I Have Promised"
"O Master, Let Me Walk with Thee"

PROPER 24
Sunday between October 16 and 22 inclusive

Gospel: Matthew 22:15-22
Theme: Allegiance to nation and to God

Call to Worship

Pastor: Allegiance to our nation is God's will; but it must not hinder our allegiance to God.

People: And allegiance to God ought not to keep us from being responsible citizens in our nation.

Pastor: Our nation deserves our loyalty. But every government is finally responsible to God. It cannot claim what belongs to God.

People: We thank God for our nation, and pledge our allegiance to it. And we reaffirm our faith in God, the final ruler of all nations.

Collect

Almighty God, who holds all nations responsible to your divine authority: Give us the conviction to be true in our allegiance, both to our nation and to you; that we may be strong in our faith, and give strength to our nation through our faith. We pray in Jesus' name. Amen.

Prayer of Confession

We love our nation, Father, and commit ourselves to its support and defense. But we would not want that allegiance to interfere with our devotion to you. Nevertheless, we interfere with it ourselves through apathy. Forgive us when we are so careless in giving you what is yours, but continue to expect you to bless our land and our lives. Make us a strong nation to people who are sincere in our devotion to you, and in our support of one another. In our Savior's name we pray. Amen.

Hymns

"God of Our Fathers"
"My Country, 'Tis of Thee"
"Once to Every Man and Nation"
"These Things Shall Be"

PROPER 25
Sunday between October 23 and 29 inclusive

First Lesson: Ruth 2:1-134
Theme: Unexpected blessings

Call to Worship
Pastor: God often surprises us with blessings we do not expect.
People: **God is so good to us! We are not worthy of his love, yet his kindness is unending.**
Pastor: God loves us, because we are a part of his family; and he wants to keep us in his care.
People: **We are happy to be a part of God's family; and want only to please him with our lives.**

Collect
Gracious God, you are so good to us when we are so unworthy of your love! Help us to accept your blessings with humility, and give our devotion with thanksgiving; that we may always be aware our happiness is the gift of your grace. In our Savior's name we pray. Amen.

Prayer of Confession
We are blessed beyond measure, O God, because of your goodness to us. But how often we are blind, and miss the joy of experiencing your unexpected kindness. Forgive us when we become obsessed with boredom and frustration instead of rejoicing in the wonder of your love. Open our eyes, and touch our hearts; that we may sing your praise, and glorify your name. Hear us for Jesus' sake. Amen.

Hymns
"All People That on Earth Do Dwell"
"Come, Let Us Tune Our Loftiest Song"
"Praise to the Lord, the Almighty"
"When All Thy Mercies, O My God"

PROPER 25
Sunday between October 23 and 29 inclusive

Second Lesson: 1 Thessalonians 2:1-8
Theme: Witnessing

Call to Worship
Pastor: God has called us to share our faith by witnessing to others.
People: We pray that others will choose Christ, and grow in their faith with the help of our witness.
Pastor: For our witness to bear fruit, we must be honest and sincere in the way we share our faith.
People: May the life we live be true to the faith we profess, and guide others in finding Christ as their Savior.

Collect
Almighty God, who shares your love with our world through the testimony of those in the household of faith: Help us to be honest and sincere in the witness we give; that others may know the truth of your love, and be set free to honor you with their lives. In Jesus' name we pray. Amen.

Prayer of Confession
We have faith, O God, and we want to share it with others. but it seems difficult at times to let others know how we feel, and what we believe. Forgive us when we do not share our faith for the spiritual enrichment of others. Help us to know how, and be willing, to share our faith with others; that the love you offer to all people will become a reality for those to whom we are sent. In the name of Christ we pray. Amen.

Hymns
"Brightly Beams Our Father's Mercy"
"I Love To Tell the Story"
"O Zion Haste"
"We've a Story to Tell to the Nations"

PROPER 25
Sunday between October 23 and 29 inclusive

Gospel: Matthew 22:34-46
Theme: The Great Commandment

Call to Worship

Pastor: God is a great God who has made all people in his own image.

People: We are the children of God, brothers and sisters to the people of all nations.

Pastor: The fatherhood of God and brotherhood of nations require us to love God above all else, and love each person as ourselves.

People: May God's grace enable us to be loving children toward God, and toward each other.

Collect

Almighty God and Father of all persons: You have stated clearly your commandment to love you with our whole being, and to love all persons as ourselves. Grant us hearts capable of expressing that kind of love; that our worship may be sincere, and our society a true family of brothers and sisters. In Jesus' name we pray. Amen.

Prayer of Confession

Gracious Father, we need you to be our God, and we need each other's love. But we are such self-loving persons, motivated by hate, prejudice, and jealousy. Forgive us for withholding our love from one another, making our devotion to a false commitment of love to you, or anyone else except ourselves. Inspire us with self-giving love; that we may become loving persons, obedient to your command. In Jesus' name we pray. Amen.

Hymns

"All Praise to Our Redeeming Lord"
"In Christ There Is No East or West"
"Lord Jesus, I Love Thee"
"More Love to Thee, O Christ"

PROPER 26
Sunday between October 30 and November 5 inclusive

First Lesson: Ruth 4:7-17
Theme: Hope restored

Call to Worship
Pastor: Life often makes us feel depressed and discouraged, but God is our source of hope.

**People: We don't expect life to treat us as special; but we
do need God to lift us up when we feel cast down.**

Pastor: Life becomes what we let it become. If we let it
become a gift of God, we will be refreshed with
new hope.

**People: Our hope is in God, whom we believe is in our midst
to make life a source of joy.**

Collect
Loving God, who turns discouragement into hope, and
despair into joy: Bless us with your presence; that we may
see each day as a gift of your love, and live in thanksgiving
for the hope that is ours in Christ Jesus, your Son, in whose
name we pray. Amen.

Prayer of Confession
Life oftens feels empty, Lord, and we suffer in our discouragement. Forgive us when we let life ruin the hope which you
have created us to enjoy. We commit ourselves to you in
the sure confidence that you will teach us how to live, and
restore hope in our hearts as we follow your will. In our
Savior's name we pray. Amen.

Hymns
"Jesus, the Very Thought of Thee"
"My Hope is Built"
"O God, Our Help in Ages Past"
"There Is a Balm in Gilead"

PROPER 26
Sunday between October 30 and November 5 inclusive

Second Lesson: 1 Thessalonians 2:9-13, 17-20
Theme: The gospel is God's message, not man's

Call to Worship
Pastor: God has spoken; but he uses the mouths of human beings to convey his message.

People: His message is the gospel: the good news of Christ who gives deliverance, rebirth, and hope.

Pastor: It is a message we hear from people like ourselves; but it is God's message, not ours.

Poeple: We love to hear the stories of Jesus, for we know it is God's word, carried by human messengers.

Collect
Eternal God, whose word is spoken to each generation with the lips of persons called to speak on your behalf: Give us hearts receptive to the gospel; that we may know we have heard your word, and not that of human origin. In Jesus' name we pray. Amen.

Prayer of Confession
We need your word, O God, but much of what we hear, we give little thought to, because it comes with human voice. Forgive us when you have used your servants to speak to us, and we have turned a deaf ear, dismissing it as thoughts of the human mind. Continue to use your servants, that we may know your word. We pray through Christ our Lord. Amen.

Hymns
"O For a Thousand Tongues to Sing"
"Pour Out Thy Spirit from on High"
"Tell Me the Stories of Jesus"
"Ye Servants of God"

208

PROPER 26
Sunday between October 30 and November 5 inclusive

Gospel: Matthew 23:1-12
Theme: Warning against hypocrisy

Call to Worship

Pastor: Commitment to the Christian faith is a way of life, not just knowledge of God's laws.

People: Many of Jesus' day knew how to look righteous without being righteous.

Pastor: Jesus condemned them for their hypocrisy, and called his followers into a life of humility and service.

People: May the devotion we feel for God in our hearts direct us to live in the beauty of holiness.

Collect

Gracious Father, who has made righteousness a way of life rather than a ritual of appearance: Create in us new hearts which will make us sincere in our expressions of faith, that our lives may demonstrate with honesty the profession of our lips. We pray through Jesus Christ our Lord. Amen.

Prayer of Confession

Forgive us, Father, for our desire to look more righteous than we are. We learn so easily how to act as Christians, and we find ourselves acting instead of living. Cleanse us of all false piety, and fill us with your Spirit to live genuine Christian lives. Hear us for Jesus' sake. Amen.

Hymns

"Breathe on Me, Breath of God"
"God Who Touchest Earth with Beauty"
"I Would Be True"
"Love Divine, All Loves Excelling"

PROPER 27
Sunday between November 6 and 12 inclusive

First Lesson: Amos 5:18-24
Theme: Call for righteousness and justice

Call to Worship

Pastor: God requires of the human race a social system of equal rights for all people.

People: Many of our brothers and sisters are wronged because of prejudice or politics or poverty.

Pastor: For these, the Church is called to be the Lord's prophetic voice: Justice and righteousness are God's will to which the human race must bow.

People: We pray for a Church to speak this word clearly; a world to hear it favorably; and a society to enjoy it peacefully.

Collect

Almighty God, who looks with displeasure on a world of social injustice: Enable your Church to be an effective servant on behalf of those who are abused by the injustice of others; that our world may move into the era of unity and peace. In the name of Christ we pray. Amen.

Prayer of Confession

The world cries, Father, and we do not hear it, because we are singing our favorite hymns too loudly in praise for our own blessings. Forgive us when we do not hear or see or cry with those who are treated less than brothers or sisters. Guide us in a ministry that will speak on behalf of those not heard; and bring equality to those who are despised. Hear us for Jesus' sake. Amen.

Hymns

"At Length There Dawns the Glorious Day"
"God Send Us Men"
"We Bear the Strain of Earthly Care"
"Where Cross the Crowded Ways of Life"

PROPER 27
Sunday between November 6 and 12 inclusive

Second Lesson: 1 Thessalonians 4:13-18
Theme: The resurrection of the dead

Call to Worship

Pastor: Jesus died and rose again, promising eternal life to all who believe in him.

People: We believe that those who have died believing in Christ, shall also be raised.

Pastor: They shall be raised to life, and be forever with our Lord.

People: Our hope is in Christ who assures us that we shall share in his resurrection.

Collect

O loving Father, who raised your Son in glory, and promised that same glory to all who believe in him: Keep us mindful of the hope you have given us in your Son; that, with our Christian friends who have gone before us in death, we may share in the resurrection of our Lord and Savior, Jesus Christ, in whose name we pray. Amen.

Prayer of Confession

Forgive us, Father, for any doubts we may hold in our minds concerning the resurrection of the dead. We are earthly beings, familiar with an earthly world, and often have difficulty comprehending all the glory of the spiritual nature you have put within us. Make our hearts glad with hope, as we share with one another our faith in the resurrection. Hear us for Jesus' sake. Amen.

Hymns

"For All the Saints"
"Jerusalem the Golden"
"Sing with All the Sons of Glory"
"The Day of Resurrection"

PROPER 27
Sunday between November 6 and 12 inclusive

Gospel: Matthew 25:1-13
Theme: Parable of the ten virgins

Call to Worship
Pastor: God offers the blessing and joy of his kingdom to all who will come to him.

People: The invitation is given; but we must prepare ourselves to be ready for his kingdom if we are to be included.

Pastor: We make ourselves ready through repentance, expecting the fulfillment of his kingdom.

People: We do not know when that will be, but we desire to be ready at all times.

Collect
O God our heavenly Father, whose kingdom is the hope of all who prepare themselves through penitence and righteousness: Keep us mindful of our responsibility to live as persons who are ready for the eternal blessing of your Son Jesus Christ, in whose name we pray. Amen.

Prayer of Confession
Life is full of happy experiences, Father, but none of them compares with the joy that awaits those who enter your kingdom. Yet we are careless and negligent with our discipleship, making ourselves unprepared to receive that joy. Forgive us when we live from day to day without thought of giving ourselves in diligent preparations. Teach us to be at our best, in readiness for our Lord and Savior, through whom we pray. Amen.

Hymns
"Joyful, Joyful, We Adore Thee"
"O Day of God, Draw Nigh"
"O Jesus, I Have Promised"
"The Lord Will Come and Not Be Slow"

PROPER 28
Sunday between November 13 and 19 inclusive

First Lesson: Zephaniah 1:7, 12-18
Theme: God's wrath on man's sin

Call to Worship

Leader: It is a high calling to be chosen by God to speak on his behalf.

Response: God has empowered us with his Spirit to speak with honest conviction his will concerning the Christian life.

Leader: The responsibility to speak is not with words only, but by example, that others may be inspired to live righteous lives.

Response: May the words we speak be illustrated by the life we live!

Collect

Almighty God, who has called your pastors to speak the truth, and to live by the truth they speak· Consecrate us in our service, that we may give honor to you in all we do. In our Savior's name we pray. Amen.

Prayer of Confession

We are sinful people, Father, and the more we sin the more we convince ourselves we are alright. We misinterpret your love thinking we may do as we please without having to face judgment. Forgive us for our indifference to the justice of your love. Help us not only to accept your love, but also the responsible life that is inspired by your love. We pray in our Savior's name. Amen.

Hymns

"Go, Make of All Disciples"
"I Would Be True"
"Let Zion's Watchmen All Awake"
"O Young and Fearless Prophet"

PROPER 28
Sunday between November 13 and 19 inclusive

Second Lesson: 1 Thessalonians 5:1-11
Theme: Be ready for Christ's return

Call to Worship

Pastor: The Day of the Lord will come as a thief in the night, without warning.

People: We who are God's children should be ready at all times, without fear.

Pastor: Instead of fear, we should be full of joy, because of our salvation in Jesus!

People: Praise God for our salvation in Christ Jesus!

Collect

Heavenly Father, who desires that we should each receive salvation through your Son: Keep us strong in our faith, and alert in our discipleship; that we may live as your children without fear of destruction, encouraged by your love. In our Savior's name we pray. Amen.

Prayer of Confession

We have faith in your Son Jesus, Father; but we need more faith to be ready for his return. Forgive us for our immaturity in living as your children, unsure of the salvation which Christ has given us. Awaken us to the joy which is ours; that we may know we are your children, saved by your Son who died for us. In his name we pray. Amen.

Hymns

"O Day of God, Draw Nigh"
"O Happy Day"
"The King Shall Come"
"The Lord Will Come and Not Be Slow"

PROPER 28
Sunday between November 13 and 19 inclusive

Gospel: Matthew 25:14-30
Theme: Parable of the three stewards

Call to Worship
Pastor: God has entrusted us with the gift of life: life which is responsible to Christ our Lord.

People: Every day we live is a day which cannot be relived. We must do our best while it is ours.

Pastor: The gift is from God. But he expects us to invest ourselves in it, that life may become more rewarding.

People: May God help us be faithful with our stewardship, as we invest our lives in the joy of his love.

Collect
Gracious Father, whose gift of life includes abilities which demand responsibility: Keep us faithful in commiting our whole being to living the Christian life, that discipleship may lead us into an ever growing and maturing experience of salvation through Christ. In his name we pray. Amen.

Prayer of Confession
Father, we want to be Christian; but to be committed is a challenge we are hardly prepared for. We have preserved our certificates of baptism and membership, but they represent little investment of our self in living Christian lives. Forgive us for being unfaithful with our stewardship as Christian disciples. Lead us by your Spirit to give our best in living as followers of Christ our Lord, through whom we pray. Amen.

Hymns
"A Charge to Keep I Have"
"Awake, Awake to Love and Work"
"Have Thine Own Way, Lord"
"Take My Life, and Let It Be Consecrated"

PROPER 29
Sunday between November 20 and 26 inclusive

First Lesson: Ezekiel 34:11-16, 20-24
Theme: God is a shepherd to his people

Call to Worship
Pastor: God is aware that his people often feel lost like sheep who have no shepherd.

People: We cannot live without divine guidance to lead us through life.

Pastor: God loves all his people, and promises to lead us like a shepherd who loves his sheep.

People: We trust in God to keep us under his protective love!

Collect
Gracious Father, who cares for your children like a faithful shepherd: Be near us in all our life situations; that we may be assured you are defending us against all that would bring us harm. We pray through Christ our Lord. Amen.

Prayer of Confession
We want to be led through life in safety, Father, but we allow ourselves to be misguided by all kinds of sinful detours. Forgive us when we let ourselves be led astray by sinful desires which are contrary to your will. Make us aware of your presence, your love, and your guidance; that we may find the joy of Christian living. In our Savior's name we pray. Amen.

Hymns
"All the Way My Savior Leads Me"
"He Leadeth Me: O Blessed Thought"
"Savior, Like a Shepherd Lead Us"
"The King of Love My Shepherd Is"

PROPER 29
Sunday between November 20 and 26 inclusive

Second Lesson: 1 Corinthians 15:20-28
Theme: Christ rules over all powers

Call to Worship

Pastor: Christ has ascended to heaven and rules over his kingdom.

People: He is King of our lives, and conquers all evil that would destroy us.

Pastor: Christ is King till the end of time. Even death is defeated by his power.

People: All hail to Christ our King! He has redeemed us to be in his kingdom forever!

Collect

Almighty God, who has given all power and authority to your Son: Grant us obedient and humble hearts; that we may be faithful and loyal followers, assured of our eternal destiny in your kingdom. We pray in the name of Christ our Lord. Amen.

Prayer of Confession

Father, forgive us for any resistance on our part to live in your kingdom with Christ ruling our lives. We desire to be obedient children; but we are motivated by independence, with a strong urge to be in charge of our lives. Give us victory over the power of evil, by our surrender to Christ our King, in whose name we pray. Amen.

Hymns

"All Hail the Power of Jesus' Name"
"All Praise to Thee, for Thou, O King Divine"
"Crown Him with Many Crowns"
"Majestic Sweetness Sits Enthroned"

PROPER 29
Sunday between November 20 and 26 inclusive

Gospel: Matthew 25:31-46
Theme: The final judgment

Call to Worship
Pastor: Our Lord comes to us through servants who witness on his behalf.
People: Many of his servants suffer with physical needs such as hunger, thirst, or sickness; and we fail to recognize our Lord.
Pastor: The Judgment, Jesus said, separates those who are receptive from those who reject our Lord's witnesses.
People: We do want to receive our Lord. May we be responsive as he speaks through the needs of our fellow men.

Collect
Almighty God, before whom we must stand in judgment: Heal the blindness of our eyes, and melt the coldness of our hearts as we hear the cries of our world, that we may know you are in our midst with the truth of redemption which will defend us in the day of Judgment. We pray through Christ our Lord. Amen.

Prayer of Confession
We would not want to be guilty of rejecting Jesus, Father; but our indifference toward human suffering accuses us of doing just that. Forgive us for ignoring our Lord by ignoring the needs of his representatives. Fill us with compassion, that our faithfulness to our world's needs will make us faithful to our Lord. In his name we pray. Amen.

Hymns
"O Brother Man, Fold to Thy Heart"
"The Voice of God Is Calling"
"We Thank Thee, Lord"
"Where Cross the Crowded Ways of Life"

ALL SAINTS' SUNDAY
(Or First Sunday in November)

First Lesson: Revelation 7:9-17
Theme: Eternal reward of the faithful

Call to Worship

Pastor: Blessed are those who are faithful to Christ in this life!

People: We celebrate the glory of those who now surround the throne of Christ, praising God!

Pastor: This world is transitory, but full of sorrow and pain. Those who endure by faith in Christ are blessed with joy forever!

People: Salvation comes from God! We praise him for the faithful who serve him, and for his faithfulness to those who trust him.

Collect

Gracious Father, whose glory is poured upon those who gave faithful service to your Son: Endow your church with conviction to be faithful in times when persecution is replaced by apathy and indifference, that we may continue to serve Christ, and become his church triumphant. In Christ's name we pray. Amen.

Prayer of Confession

Praised be your name, O God, for you have remained faithful in every generation! Glory and honor is yours for the mighty deliverance you have given to those who commit their ways to you. With the gift of your Son, you have opened the blessing of eternity to all who will believe. Accept us as those who believe, forgiving us for our sins. Cleanse us of unrighteousness, that we may join the chorus which forever sings your praises. Hear us for Christ's sake. Amen.

Hymns

"Angel Voices, Ever Singing"
"For All the Saints"
"Look, Ye Saints! The Sight Is Glorious"

ALL SAINTS' SUNDAY
(Or the First Sunday in November)

Second Lesson: 1 John 3:1-3
Theme: We shall be like him

Call to Worship

Pastor: God loves us so much that he calls us his children!

People: God is, and always will be, our Father. But we do not know what we shall be like after death.

Pastor: We know that when we see Jesus, we shall be like him!

People: That is our hope, and it motivates us to keep ourselves pure for our Lord.

Collect

Almighty God, whose love is without end to those who call you Father: Help us to live like Jesus as much as we possibly can; that we may continue in your love even into eternity where we shall be like Jesus, in whose name we pray. Amen.

Prayer of Confession

We are your children because of your great love, Father. And we look forward to the glories of eternity. But we struggle with our attempts to be pure. Forgive us our sins which keep us impure. Cleanse us with Christ's purity; that, in eternity, sin may no longer mar the image you have given us. We pray through Christ our Lord. Amen.

Hymns

"Blest Are the Pure in Heart"
"Give Me the Wings of Faith"
"Happy the Souls to Jesus Joined"
"Rejoice, Ye Pure in Heart"

ALL SAINTS' SUNDAY
(Or First Sunday in November)

Gospel: Matthew 5:1-12
Theme: The Beatitudes

Call to Worship

Pastor: Many saints suffered humiliation when they served our Lord. But now they enjoy his glory in eternal bliss.

People: We are not without example in living consecrated lives for our Lord.

Pastor: If we are faithful, we, too, shall enjoy God's glory, as it begins in this life and continues into the next.

People: Praise God for all his saints! By their witness we are inspired with faithfulness.

Collect

Eternal Father, who blesses forever those who are faithful to you: Inspire us by the example of the saints who have gone before us and are now in your eternal care; that we may serve you with steadfastness, and know the happiness of faithfulness. In the name of Christ we pray. Amen.

Prayer of Confession

We are sure of joys forever which you give your Saints in glory, Father. But we are less sure of the joy which belongs to this life. Forgive us when our service, as well as our joy, has been hindered by our fear of suffering and ignorance of true happiness. Give us courage, and conviction, to be true to our Christian nature; that we, too, may share in your eternal joy. We pray in our Savior's name. Amen.

Hymns

"Blest Are the Pure in Heart"
"For All the Saints"
"Give Me the Wings of Faith"

THANKSGIVING

First Lesson: Deuteronomy 8:7-18
Theme: Give thanks for a fertile land

Call to Worship
Pastor: God has blessed us once again with a rich harvest.
People: **We are always amazed at the way our land produces. Even when crops fail, we still have plenty to eat.**
Pastor: God is the reason for our blessings. To him we lift our prayers fo thanksgiving, and offerings of praise.
People: **Thanks be to God for another rich harvest that assures us of food, strength, and health!**

Collect
Almighty God, you have blessed our soil with sun, and rain, and fertility. We give you thanks for the fertile land by which we are fed; and pray that the bounty of our land will be used to feed not just ourselves, but those who know the pain of humger. In our Savior's name we pray. Amen.

Prayer of Confession
We are grateful for our harvest, O God. You have blessed us in abundance; and we still will be well nourished. But our thanksgiving is not without the murmurs of our human nature when we worry about high prices, or brag about technology. Forgive us when we compromise our thankfulness wit self-pity, or self-praise. Open our eyes to see your love; open our lips to praise your love; and open our hearts to share your love. In the name of Christ we pray. Amen.

Hymns
"As Men of Old Their First Fruits Brought"
"Come, Ye Thankful People, Come"
"To Thee, O Lord, Our Hearts We Raise"
"We Plow the Fields"

THANKSGIVING

Second Lesson: 2 Corinthians 9:6-15
Theme: Give others a reason to be thankful

Call to Worship

Pastor: Thankfulness is a personal response each one makes to God in appreciation for his goodness.

People: We come to God with thanksgiving, because he has been so generous with us.

Pastor: Others would share our gratitude to God, if we would share the blessings of God with them.

People: May our thankfulness be genuine enough to make us generous enough to share with others; that they too, will give thanks to God.

Collect

Gracious God, out of your generosity you have showered us with kindness. Share with us your generous spirit; that we may share with others our blessings. Thus may all your people join together in songs of praise and thanksgiving for your benevolent kindness. In Jesus' name we pray. Amen.

Prayer of Confession

We feel blessed, O God, because you are so good to us. But we become selfish with these blessings, and believe those who have less, are just less fortunate. Forgive us when we allow fortune to be bad for some, and your gifts to be possessed by others. Produce a rich harvest in our world through the generosity of your followers; that many will give thanks for your goodness. In the name of Christ we pray. Amen.

Hymns

"All People That on Earth Do Dwell"
"Lift Up Our Hearts, O King of Kings"
"Now Thank We All Our God"
"O Brother Man, Fold to Thy Heart"

THANKSGIVING

Gospel: Luke 17:11-19
Theme: Thank God for your blessings

Call to Worship

Pastor: Each day of our lives, God touches us with his love.
People: We are blessed beyond our expectations. God is so good!
Pastor: God is faithful with his goodness. We should be just as faithful with our gratitude.
People: May the way we live be a daily prayer of thanksgiving to God for his goodness.

Collect

Loving God, you deserve a continual prayer of thanksgiving for all your goodness to us! Keep our hearts and minds sensitive to your generosity; that we may always be in communion with you to express our gratitude. In our Savior's name we pray. Amen.

Prayer of Confession

We praise you, O God, for the many gifts of your love which you give so freely. You have given so much that we find ourselves expecting your benevolence. Forgive us when we have taken our blessings for granted, only to ask for more. Put a spirit of gratitude within us; that we may accept each gift with a prayer of thanksgiving. In Jesus' name we pray. Amen.

Hymns

"Come, Ye Thankful People, Come"
"For All the Blessings of the Year"
"How Great Thou Art"
"Now Thank We All Our God"

Index of Scriptures

TOPICAL INDEX